THE DEVELOPMENT AND PRACTICE OF CORPORATE GOVERNANCE IN ZAMBIA

Successes and Challenges

PATRICK D. CHISANGA

PENSULO | LUSAKA

Published in Lusaka by Pensulo Publishers Limited
©Patrick D. Chisanga, 2019

ISBN: 978-9982-952-19-4

Copy Editing by Marita Banda
Cover Design, Typesetting & Layout by Victor Phiri
Publishing Project Manager: George Arudo
Publisher: Chanda Penda

pensulopublishers@zambia.co.zm
www.facebook.com/PensuloPublishers
+260979443150

Pensulo books are distributed worldwide

TABLE OF CONTENTS

PART A
THE DEVELOPMENT OF CORPORATE GOVERNANCE IN ZAMBIA

PART B
THE PRACTICE OF CORPORATE GOVERNANCE

V

PREFACE

This book has four important missions; firstly, to reflect on the background and origins of Corporate Governance in Zambia. Secondly, to review the development on Corporate Governance practices over the last 25 years. Thirdly, to vision the way forward for Corporate Governance in the Zambian Economy and fourthly, to serve as a ready reference resource for corporate governance practitioners and students alike.

It is hoped that such an analysis will contribute positively to the development and growth of sound Corporate Governance practices in both the public and the private sectors of Zambia.

The seed to commence writing this book was planted in me by Michael Gillibrand, a colleague in Corporate Governance work, about whom I will say a little more later. Michael Gillibrand had just retired from the Commonwealth Secretariat in London when he came to Southern Africa as a Corporate Governance Consultant. I had just concluded my three-year term as President of the Institute of Directors (IoD) Zambia when Michael came to pay a courtesy call on me at my office in Lusaka.

During our hour long meeting, we reflected over a wide range of Corporate Governance developments in Southern Africa, and in Zambia in particular. At the conclusion of our meeting, Michael Gillibrand had this to say, "Patrick, I think you should seriously consider writing a book on Corporate Governance in Zambia, because I believe that you, more than anyone else, has been closest to the subject over the years." I promised Michael that I would give his suggestion serious thought when I have had sufficient time to gather my thinking.

I felt compelled to write this book for two good reasons; firstly, in all my research work, I have come to observe that so far, there is no book to my knowledge that has been written on the subject of Corporate Governance in Zambia to date.

Secondly, I have come to believe that there is a strong correlation between sound Corporate Governance practices and the levels of economic advancement attained by various countries all over the world. This is particularly true with regard to the emerging economies from the third world. I have observed for example, that in our sub-region, countries that have attained higher levels of Corporate Governance reform, such as South Africa, Mauritius, Botswana, Namibia and Mozambique are also exhibiting growing levels of investor confidence and economic growth.

I have also observed that good corporate Governance has become a necessary lever in creating efficient companies, organisations and business enterprises capable of creating wealth and employment, alleviating poverty, enhancing the standard and quality of life of the people, and thus generally contributing to positive economic growth and development.

Against this background, it is my hope that this book will contribute, even in a small way, to raising the bar of Corporate Governance principles and practices in Zambia, which will result into enhanced levels of economic advancement in the country.

Significant strides in Corporate Governance reforms in Zambia have been achieved since the launch of the Corporate Governance Campaign in Zambia in the year 2000, but quite clearly, much more needs to be done.

ACKNOWLEDGEMENTS

This book would not have been possible without the support, encouragement and assistance from a number of people.

I have already observed in the Preface to this book that the seed to start writing the book was planted in me by Mr. Michael Gillibrand, a colleague in Corporate Governance. Unfortunately I have since completely lost track of him, but I believe he is in England, somewhere. Wherever you are in the world at this time Michael, please know that, I have finally fulfilled the dream you had ignited in me.

I am particularly grateful to Mr. Kunda E. Kalaba a member of the initial task force of June 1998, who now lives and works in Singapore, for allowing me access to his invaluable and copious notes covering what transpired at the three day workshop held at Intercontinental Hotel in Lusaka from the 22nd to the 24th June 1998, at which the decision to commence working towards the establishment of the Institute of Directors of Zambia was taken. I had promised Mr. Kalaba that I would acknowledge his contribution once my book is finally published.

I would also like to acknowledge the tremendous moral encouragement that I received from my daughter, Mubanga when she was a student at the University of the District of Colombia UDC, in Washington, DC. Every time I visited her, during my sessions at the IFC's Global Corporate Governance Forum, we discussed Corporate Governance passionately. In February 2009, she bought me a book on Corporate Governance by Colin Coulson - Thomas, in which she wrote, "This is my small contribution to your remarkable work in Corporate Governance ..." I still draw inspiration in my work from that note.

Another source of inspiration has been my nephew, Dr. Conrad Mbewe, a Senior Pastor in the Baptist Church. Conrad has written several books on Theology and Christianity in his area of calling over the last few years. When he came to present me with his latest book, I told him that before his next book is published, I will have written my first book in my area of specialisation, Corporate Governance! Conrad, I have now delivered on my undertaking. Thank you for inspiring me to start writing.

Over the last 40 odd years, I have served on many Boards in both the private and the public sectors in Zambia and abroad. On most of the Boards that I have served, I have often learnt something new, from my fellow Directors. I would like to thank all these colleagues for freely sharing with me their knowledge and experiences. I do hope that over the years, I have done justice to the many insights that I have gained from them.

I am especially grateful to my Personal Assistant, Margaret Mukondwa, for working tirelessly to type and retype the manuscript until we had it right. I should also like to express and record a word of thanks to our Head of Marketing at my Consulting Firm Dynamic Concepts Limited, Clement Mwamba, for the meticulous research work that he carried out throughout the final preparatory stages of the typescript.

In closing I should like to record a word of thanks to Mrs. Victoria Silutongwe, current Institute of Directors (IoD) Zambia President for the painstaking reviewing that she undertook in the final stages of the typescript. Elsewhere in the book, I have reflected on Victoria's unique dedication to the IoD having risen from Administration Officer to President over a period of almost 20 years!

The professional approach and support I received from the team members of Pensulo Publishers Ltd was very instrumental in transforming the script into publishable and marketable product that it is today.

Finally, I owe a very special debt of gratitude to my wife Petronella for her support, understanding and endurance as I worked many long hours in my study.

Often she would not fall asleep because of the light streaming through, since my study in our home is adjacent to our bedroom! Throughout the process, she also served as my constitutional advisor as I worked on the manuscript.

Patrick D. Chisanga FCG, FIoDZ
Lusaka
Zambia
December, 2019.

FOREWORD

After years of many people asking whether the Institute of Directors (IoD) Zambia had any documents that outlined the history of the Institute, we now have a book that documents this from inception. This book is not only timely but is highly informative and a good read. I have had some questions of who the trail blazers were and how they set out to establish the Institute. This book has clarified a lot of gray areas.

Mr. Patrick Chisanga is one of the trail blazers and so writes from the position of what he did, saw and experienced as they established the Institute of Directors. He later served as the second President of the IoD. The author has further continued to offer training in corporate governance and has continued to be a member (in good standing) of the institute.

Patrick provides much needed background information on the IoD and its long-term collaboration with organisations such as the Institute of Chartered Secretaries and Administrators (ICSA), The Global Corporate Governance Forum (GCGF) and the African Corporate Governance Network (ACGN). Further, the author gives us a wonderful summary of what corporate governance is, its challenges in practice and benefits when there is adherence. Simply put; as Directors we need to uphold good corporate practices by walking the talk.

I am privileged to have participated in training with the author of this very important book which provides essential information. We often hear that "if it is not written down, it is probably because it doesn't exist." Now we have the facts on IoD Zambia and how we got to where we are. A must read!

Prof. Esther Munalula Nkandu
President Institute of Directors of Zambia
2016 - 2019

A BRIEF OVERVIEW

This is the first effort, by an expert, to write a book on the Development and Growth of Corporate Governance in Zambia. The book is divided into two sections:

Part A – Historical Perspective and Part B – Corporate Governance and its challenges in Practice. Part A gives a direct account of what transpired when a small group of dedicated Zambians, not more than 17, worked tirelessly as a Task Force from June, 1998, to prepare for the establishment of the Institute of Directors of Zambia. This book's author was the Chairman of the Task Force and the historical recollections outlined in the book are therefore authentic.

Part B delves into Corporate Governance, from its definition to its practice among the private sector companies and the State Owned Enterprises (SOEs). A whole chapter in the book is dedicated to discussing the complexities that are found in SOEs and how Corporate Governance should still be applied in order that SOEs are run efficiently and profitably.

The author does not claim to say the last word on Corporate Governance in Zambia but concludes that, **"A lot more remains to be done."** More Zambians are therefore urged to come forward and write on this very exciting subject of Corporate Governance.

Amb. Mumba S. Kapumpa, SC, FIoDZ
Corporate Governance Consultant
Past President IoDZ (2007 – 2009)

ABOUT THE AUTHOR

PATRICK DANIEL CHISANGA - ABRIDGED PROFILE.

Patrick D. Chisanga is a Fellow of the Chartered Governance Institute (UK), from the London School of Accountancy. He is a Chartered Governance Professional. He is also a Fellow of the Institute of Directors of Zambia and a member of the Institute of Directors of Southern Africa.

He spent nearly 20 years in the Public and Corporate sectors of Zambia, serving as Chief Executive and as Chairman of many organisations and companies before he took early retirement in 1994, to focus on running his own family held Group of Companies, under Muchanga Investments Limited, which he had founded in 1987 and serves as Chairman.

He is also Chairman and Lead Consultant of Dynamic Concepts Limited, a consultancy firm which undertakes Corporate Governance Consulting, Leadership Development and Personal Motivational Development in Zambia the Southern African Region and Africa as a whole.

He is the Founder current Chairperson of Zambian Institute of Leadership.

He has made many presentations on Corporate Governance in countries of the Southern and West African Region, including Mozambique, South Africa, Malawi, Zimbabwe, Namibia, Nigeria and his home country, Zambia.

In August, 2014, he was appointed by the Zambian Government to serve as Director General of the Zambia Development Agency, ZDA. ZDA is charged with the responsibility of promoting and facilitating Zambia's Economic growth and Development.

He currently serves on the boards of several local and international companies and corporate organisations either as Chairman or non-Executive Director.

He served as Chairman of Air Namibia, Zambia Ltd from November, 2009 to December, 2019.

He is a member of the Advisory Council of the Namibia Institute of Corporate Governance, NICG.

He currently serves as a Board Member of ECOBANK Foundation.

He previously served as Advisor to Konkola Copper Mines Ltd, KCM, Zambia's largest Copper Mining Company, from 2009 to 2013.

He served as Advisor to Skorpion Zinc Mines of Namibia from 2010 to 2014.

He is a Founder Member and a Fellow of the Institute of Directors of Zambia where he served as President for three years from 2002 to 2005.

He is a Past Chairman of the Institute of Chartered Secretaries and Administrators in Zambia. He is Past Vice Chairman of the Economics Association of Zambia.

He is a Past Governor of Rotary International District 9210, comprising: Zambia, Zimbabwe, Malawi and Northern Mozambique.

He served as International Training Leader of Rotary International from 2006 to 2008.

In February, 2014, he was appointed by the President of Republic Zambia to serve as a member of the Legal and Justice Reforms Commission of the Republic of Zambia.

In April, 2018, he was appointed Chairman of the Board of Directors of the Lusaka South Multi-Facility Economic Zone, a key instrument of Zambia's industrialisation and economic diversification strategy.

He has served as Chairman of Rotary International in Africa. In this capacity, his mandate was to co-ordinate Rotary's Development and Humanitarian Work on the African Continent.

He is a former member of the Board of Directors of the Commonwealth Association of Corporate Governance (CACG).

He has served as a member of the Global Corporate Governance Forum Private Sector Advisory Group of the World Bank.

He served as President of the Lusaka Golf Club, Zambia's premier golf club from 1999 to 2001. He remains a keen golfer and currently serves as a Trustee of the Lusaka Golf Club

In April, 2019, he was appointed by the Government of the Republic of Zambia to serve as Secretary of the National Dialogue Forum, which had been enacted to facilitate the review Constitutional Amendments to the Republican Constitution of 2016, the Public Order Act of 1955, the Electoral Process Act as well as the Political Parties Bill of 2019.

PART A
THE DEVELOPMENT OF CORPORATE GOVERNANCE IN ZAMBIA

CHAPTER 1

BACKGROUND

CORPORATE GOVERNANCE DEFINED

According to the Cadbury Report of 1992, *"Governance is the manner in which power is exercised in the management of economic and social resources for sustainable human development."*

Governance has in the last 30 years assumed critical global importance. It is a vital ingredient in the maintenance of a dynamic balance between the need for order and equality in society, the efficient production and delivery of goods and services, accountability in the use of power, the protection of human rights and freedom, and, the maintenance of an organised corporate framework within which each citizen can contribute fully towards finding innovative solutions to common problems.

"Corporate governance, on the other hand, refers to the manner in which the power of an organisation is exercised in the stewardship of the organisation's total portfolio of assets and resources with the objective of maintaining and increasing shareholder value with the satisfaction of other stakeholders in the context of the organisation's mission and objectives."
(Cadbury Report 1992)

In the Cadbury Report 1992, Corporate Governance has further been defined as the *"system by which organisations are governed, managed and controlled."*

Drawing from the above definitions good Corporate Governance seeks to promote the following ideals:

1

1. Efficient, effective and sustainable organisations that contribute to the welfare of society by creating wealth, employment and solutions to emerging challenges.

2. Responsible and accountable organisations.

3. Legitimate organisations that are managed with integrity, probity and transparency.

4. Recognition and protection of stakeholders rights.

5. Development of good corporate citizens exercising sound corporate social responsibility.

THE OECD PRINCIPLES OF CORPORATE GOVERNANCE STATES:

"Corporate governance involves a set of relationships between a company's management, its board, its shareholders and other stakeholders. Corporate governance also provides the structure through which the objectives of the company are set, and the means of attaining those objectives and monitoring performance are determined."

From the foregoing definitions by the named renowned authorities on Corporate Governance one can summarise that good corporate governance consists of a system of structuring, operating and controlling an organisation in such a way that the following outcomes are achievable.

1. A culture of checks and balances based on a foundation of sound principles and business ethics.

2. Fulfilling the long term goals of the shareholders while taking into account the expectations of all the other key stakeholders including the interests of employees past, present and future.

3. Maintaining proper compliance with all applicable legal and regulatory requirements under which the organisation is carrying out its activities.

(G20/OECD Report (2015)

There is little doubt that the application of sound corporate governance practices and principles will result in better and more efficient companies and organisations which will in turn lead to stronger economies.

These are the focal issues that I will be discussing as we look at the development of Corporate Governance in Zambia.

HISTORICAL PERSPECTIVE OF CORPORATE GOVERNANCE IN ZAMBIA

Prior to the year 1991, which is the year during which Multiparty Democracy was re-ushered onto the Zambian Sociopolitical scene, over 80% of the Zambian Economy was state controlled through the Parastatal system. The Parastatal sector embraced a large collection of companies in which the Government held a controlling interest. These included companies under the Zambia Industrial and Mining Corporation Limited (ZIMCO) group such as the Industrial Development Corporation (INDECO); the National Import and Export Corporation (NIEC); National Hotels and most of the Statutory State Owned Enterprises. Virtually every significant Company fell under the Parastatal Sector. Only about 20% of the corporate landscape was held in private hands. These were largely local entities of international Companies and multinationals such as the Lonrho Group, and International banks.

In the Parastatal Sector, the major shareholder was GRZ Plc, the Government of the Republic of Zambia. All appointments to the Boards of Directors were directly made by the state. Cabinet Ministers and Permanent Secretaries were often appointed as Chairpersons of Parastatal Boards.

ZIMCO

The Zambia Industrial and Mining Corporation ZIMCO, a holding company for all Zambian state interests, was one of the largest corporate entities in sub-Saharan Africa. It controlled over 110 principal companies relating to every major industrial activity in Zambia, including mining, consumer goods manufacturing, finance, transportation, agriculture, energy, and hoteliery. A product of Zambia's far-reaching nationalisation programme since its independence from Great Britain in 1964, ZIMCO dominated the nation's economy.

Although ZIMCO was incorporated in 1970, its beginning date back a decade earlier to a company created by the colonial Northern Rhodesian government. The Industrial Development Corporation of Zambia Ltd.

(INDECO), as it was called, attempted to energise the colony's industry, which lagged behind that of neighboring southern Rhodesia. With only limited success, INDECO vacillated between state and private control. It finally re-emerged as a stat-owned company in August 1964, just as the colony was on the brink of independence.
(Taylor Karen, 26th March 1990)

The Board of the apex State Owned Enterprise ZIMCO was actually chaired by no lesser person than the President of the Republic of Zambia himself.

All chief executives were appointed and fired by the state often at a presidential press conference.

There were hardly any Board Charters nor Codes of Corporate Governance. The performance of the Board and Directors was never evaluated. Board tenure solely depended on one's loyalty to the appointing authority. The State President and Ministers exercised a free hand in the day to day operations of Companies, particularly so with regard to Parastatal Companies. In short, the practice of Sound Corporate Governance Principles in Zambia prior to 1991 was either nonexistent or very much compromised

CORPORATE GOVERNANCE OF SOE'S IN ZAMBIA
Zambia was a socialist oriented country prior to 1991. Most of the economy was in state hands, as I have already pointed out.

The period prior to 1991 was characterised by a heavy predominance of state-owned enterprises (SOE's) often referred to as Parastatal Organisations. Estimates put the share of SOE's in industrial activity at about 80% with the private sector taking up the remaining 20%. The SOE's span virtually all sectors of the economy notably mining, Energy, Industry, Manufacturing, Agriculture, Transport and Communications, Trade, Tourism and Construction.

In the Zambian context, therefore, the term parastatal or SOE is used to refer to a public enterprise (i.e. state-owned) which is quasi-autonomous and outside the regular civil service structure. This category comprises companies

4

of a purely commercial nature set up under Cap 686 of the Laws of Zambia – the Companies Act; and also those on the list just referred to above, i.e. statutory boards and companies established by Act of Parliament.

The emergence of state participation in the commercial sector dates back to the 1968 Economic Reforms – otherwise referred to as the "Mulungushi Reforms" (named after the location, Mulungushi Rock, in Kabwe at which the policy pronouncement by President Kaunda was made).

THE MULUNGUSHI ECONOMIC REFORMS (1968)

A major switch in the structure of Zambia's economy came with the Mulungushi Reforms of April 1968: the government declared its intention to acquire equity holdings (usually 51% or more) in a number of key foreign-owned firms, to be controlled by a parastatal conglomerate named the Industrial Development Corporation (INDECO). By January 1970, Zambia had acquired majority holding in the Zambian operations of the two major foreign mining corporations, the Anglo American and the Rhodesia Selection Trust (RST); the two became the Nchanga Consolidated Copper Mines (NCCM) and Roan Consolidated Mines (RCM), respectively. The Zambian government then created a new parastatal body, the Mining Development Corporation (MINDECO). The Finance and Development Corporation (FINDECO) allowed the Zambian government to gain control of insurance companies and building societies. However, foreign-owned banks (such as Barclays, Standard Chartered and Grindlays) successfully resisted takeover. In 1971, INDECO, MINDECO, and FINDECO were brought together under an omnibus parastatal, the Zambia Industrial and Mining Corporation (ZIMCO), to create one of the largest companies in sub-Saharan Africa, with the country's president, Kenneth Kaunda as Chairman of the Board. The management contracts under which day-to-day operations of the mines had been carried out by Anglo American and RST were ended in 1973. In 1982 NCCM and RCM were merged into the giant Zambia Consolidated Copper Mines Limited.

(The World Factbook, retrieved 25th February, 2018)

Matero Reforms (1969)

Nationalisation of the Zambian mines began with the Matero declaration of 1969, when the government obtained a 51% shareholding in the then two existing mining companies. These were Roan Selection Trust and Anglo American Corporation, which owned all the operating mines in the country between them. Prior to the Matero declarations, the government had issued the Mulungushi declarations, under which 51% of the shares in all the major industries (except mines) were put in state hands. This led to the formation of INDECO as the holding company for these shares. The Matero reforms resulted in the formation of a holding company for the mines' shares to be called MINDECO. An umbrella company for MINDECO and INDECO was called Zambia Industrial and Mining Corporation (ZIMCO). Roan Selection Trust became Roan Consolidated Copper Mines (RCM), comprising Mufurila, Luanshya, Chibuluma, Chambishi, Kalengwa, and Ndola Copper Refinery. The Zambian arm of Anglo American Corporation became Nchanga Consolidated Copper Mines (NCCM) and was in charge of Rhokana, Nchanga, and Konkola mines.

The Matero reforms were implemented in January, 1970 and the government was to pay for those shares over a period of roughly 10 years. However, in 1973, the government decided to redeem all the outstanding bonds and made the following changes in the management structure, MINDECO was no longer in charge of RCM and NCCM, but other small mines in the Country. INDECO, MINDECO, RCM, and NCCM all fell under the management of an overarching parastatal, the Zambia Industrial and Mining Corporation (ZIMCO). All the managing directors of RCM and NCCM as well as the chairman of ZIMCO were political appointees. The Minister of Mines was the chairman of RCM, NCCM, and ZIMCO. In the same year, the country changed its constitution and became a one-party state
(J. Sikamo et al, June, 2016)

The nationalisation pronouncement of 1968 resulted in the state assuming 51 per cent ownership in some twenty-five companies mostly in manufacturing, transport, distribution and construction which were now brought under the umbrella of INDECO, a state-owned organisation which had been set up essentially as an instrument for stimulating industrial development. It must be stressed that the role of INDECO in the pre-1965 period was limited to that of promotion and finance of industrial ventures. The advent of state-owned enterprises with the takeovers of 1968 saw INDECO assume new, wider roles of a holding company and shareholder.

The organisation was now to play a pivotal role in initiating industrial ventures as well as overseeing the operations of subsidiary companies. Supervision of SOEs was centralised and exercised through sector group companies, FINDECO, MINDECO etc.

By the late 1980s to early 1990s the Zambian Government could no longer sustain the inefficiencies and the cost of running SOEs which was reflected in low or negligible reinvestment in most SOEs. As a result of this situation, the Government embarked on a privatisation programme starting in 1991 in order to fully divest its interest in SOEs.

In order to assume closer control of SOE's a decision was taken to dissolve ZIMCO Limited on 31st March, 1995 and the establishment of the Directorate of State Enterprises (DOSE) on 1st April, 1995. The rationale behind the creation of DOSE was to create a team of competent staff to assist the Minister of Finance to effectively monitor and supervise SOEs. This function was to be undertaken in liaison with Zambia Privatisation Agency (ZPA).

DOSE was created to manage the transition of the privatisation and commercialisation of SOEs and act as a surrogate shareholder in SOEs.

The legal status of the Directorate of State Enterprises was derived from the provisions of the Minister of Finance (Incorporation) Act CAP 588 of the Laws of Zambia.

THE FUNCTIONS OF DOSE WERE: TO

1. Act as an agent of the shareholding Minister in matters pertaining to the efficient and effective supervision of the Government's interest in SOEs;

2. Forecast, collect and record receipts of dividends from SOEs;

3. Monitor the performance of SOEs by receiving and analysing periodic financial and qualitative information from SOEs and comparing this with performance indicators;

4. Report to the shareholding Minister and other relevant organisations on the performance of the SOEs and recommend appropriate actions. Monitor the implementation of such actions once approved;

5. Ensure that all SOEs, conclude Annual General Meetings (AGM) within the time stipulated in the Companies' Act;

6. Approve the Annual Reports of each SOE during AGMs;

7. Assist in the privatisation of SOEs by providing administrative machinery;

8. Assist in commercialisation of Government departments.

DOSE was meant to reduce its staffing levels in line with the decreasing responsibilities until it could be finally phased out upon completion of the privatisation programme.

However, there was a policy change in Government which stated that some SOEs were not going to be privatised immediately, but were going to be commercialised then privatised later on.

Further, the cost of running DOSE had become unmanageable and liquidations of SOEs were taking too long to conclude. As a result, DOSE was abolished in 1999 and its functions were fused in the Ministry of Finance under the Investments and Debt Management Department (IDM).

ROLE OF SOEs

SOEs continue to play an important role in the Zambian economy in terms of employment creation, contribution to government revenues through taxes and GDP.

The surviving SOEs operate in a range of industries including; energy, communications, transportation, mining and media. These were some of the largest formal sector employers. These include ZESCO, ZAMTEL, Zambia Railways, ZCCM Investment Holdings, Zambia National Broadcasting Corporation, to name some of them.

Mode of Supervision and Monitoring of SOEs

The system entailed Dual Supervision between the shareholder ministry and the line ministry. The functional distinction between the roles of the shareholder ministry and line ministry is as follows; the shareholder ministry deals with financial oversight, appointment of Board Members (for those SOEs directly under the ministry). It also ensures participation at the Annual General Meetings. While the line ministry handles the day to day matters involving policy and technical supervision. It also appoints Board Members for SOEs directly under the line ministry.

Parliament

Parliament exercises some oversight through receipt of annual reports and deliberations of Parliamentary Committees.

Challenges Associated with the Governance of SOEs

In general Government and SOEs have faced a number of challenges which include the following:

1. The participants in the system had confusing roles and accountabilities.
2. There was no strong focus on SOE ownership and governance.
3. Units that supervised SOEs were focused on policy and regulation, not on being an effective shareholder or ensuring the state derives the most benefit from its assets.
4. Not getting the best return for its investment. Some SOEs continued to perform poorly.
5. Many SOEs were unprofitable and a significant drain on the national budget.
6. Company monitoring was carried out mainly through board attendance, and little information was centrally available.

7. While some SOEs regularly produced annual reports available to the public, much of the state-owned sector was opaque.

8. SOEs generally did not have explicit objectives, targets, or performance monitoring for their boards or management.

9. While boards had improved in recent years, some companies continued to suffer from specific problems, such as the absence of a board or CEO for extended periods.

10. Ownership functions in SOEs were shared between the Ministry of Finance and an "administrative" Ministry assigned to the SOE based on sector.

11. One consequence of this system of shared responsibilities was the duplication of duties between the shareholding ministry and the line ministry leading to poor supervision of SOEs.

12. There was lack of specific legislation or guidelines on Operations and supervision of SOEs.

SOE Governance Reforms

In recent years, Government of Zambia introduced governance reform measures aimed at improving performance. These included:

At SOE level

1. Civil servants were no longer being appointed to chair Boards of SOES.

2. Board members were drawn from the private sector on a professional basis.

3. Amendments of articles of association.

4. Implementation of Corporate Governance Practices e.g. establishment of audit committees, and other committees of the board.

At National Level

An Inter-Ministerial Committee was formed by the Secretary to the Cabinet to come up with modalities of setting up an SOE Agency.

It was in the light of the foregoing and taking cognisance of the fact that SOEs will continue to play an important role in the Zambian economy that President Michael Sata decided in 2012, to take the landmark step to transfer all SOEs from direct government administration to a new corporate entity to be known as the Industrial Development Corporation, IDC.

SUMMARY

As defined at the beginning of this chapter, Corporate Governance is a system by which organisations are governed, managed and controlled. This chapter, I believe, has helped the reader to gain a deeper appreciation of what constitutes corporate governance.

The historical perspective of Corporate Governance in Zambia which gives a detailed analysis of the status of corporate governance which existed in the country prior to the year 1991 has been outlined. Detailed information regarding the major activities and events that were undertaken which stifled good corporate governance at the time, for example, the Mulungushi Reforms which marked a major departure in the structure of Zambia's economy where the government declared its intention to acquire equity holding in a number of key foreign firms. The Matero Reforms which resulted in the formation of a holding company for the mining sector which was called MINDECO has also been chronicled.

CHAPTER 2

PRIVATISATION: POLICY FRAMEWORK

As discussed in the preceding chapter, over the years there had been general dissatisfaction over the performance of SOEs.

While it was acknowledged that parastatals in Zambia had scored some successes in the areas of industry, their general levels of efficiency left much to be desired especially on account of their vulnerability to political interference.

The turning point in terms of direct articulation of policy on privatisation came at the 5th National Convention of the United National Independence Party (UNIP) held from 14 to 17 March, 1990. At this forum, the then President of Zambia, Dr. Kenneth Kaunda, emphasised the importance of promoting entrepreneurial development and the need to create private sector competition for parastatals.

At this same forum, the Committee's deliberations on the economy addressed the issue of privatisation in serious terms. In the resolution, the convention were of the view that: "no national interests are threatened by opening up of any public enterprises to direct and limited individual private citizen full or part ownership (*Resolutions of Economic Affairs Committee, 5th National Convention of UNIP – March, 1990*).

There was a gradual build of some national consensus on the need for a fundamental shift from the entrenched policy of direct state participation in commercial activity. As a prelude to the landmark pronouncement of

May, 1990, President Kaunda on 19 April, reviewed the major considerations of state participation as conceived in 1968 as being:

1. Lack of Zambian entrepreneurs;

2. Desire to breakup monopoly pricing cartels;

3. Concern about the predominance of foreign investors with no commitment to development of host economy.

Having reviewed the state of the economy since 1968, the view of government was that the programme of state involvement had run its course and that it was time for change. The pronouncement of May 28, 1990 set Zambia on the course towards dismantling state-owned enterprises. It was announced that government had decided to: "Devolve more economic power to the Zambian people through a scheme by which the state will sell part of its capital in state enterprises to the general public," (Dr. Kaunda's address to 5th Extra Ordinary National Council).

The privatisation programme as pronounced then was to see the state offer up to 40 per cent and 49 per cent of shareholding in the following categories of industries respectively:

(a) Public Utilities

(b) Mining, Industrial and Commercial

The basic objectives of the new policy were to, "give economic power to the people." In addition, the following broad benefits were anticipated:

1. Wider distribution of wealth;

2. Supplementation of incomes of shareholders;

3. Raising revenue for government from sale of shares;

4. Improvement in quality of corporate governance.

The Government was also to arrange for the setting up of a stock exchange to facilitate public participation in ownership of companies.

As a follow up to the May, 1990 statement, the Budget Address of 16 November, 1990 reinforced government's stand on privatisation - by indicating that outright sale of SOEs was in the offing.

The new MMD Government which came in after the general elections of October, 1991, proposed economic liberalisation as the main thrust of economic recovery programme and the privatisation programme was to be a cornerstone of the strategy. At a meeting with heads of foreign missions on 5 December, 1991, the Second Republican President of Zambia, Fredrick Chiluba, stated that the new government was totally committed to privatisation and disengaging government from direct involvement in commercial activity. The MMD Government's view was that privatisation would be total and there would be "no sacred lambs."

The Budget Speech of January, 1992, gave a clear delineation of government's overall economic philosophy and its perspective on the roles of public and commercial sectors. Government was to revert to the normal role of providing public infrastructure and services and ensuring a sound fiscal and legal and economic environment. It was clearly stated that the privatisation programme was to proceed expeditiously.

The processing of the disposal of the first tranche of SOEs had to be put on hold with the ushering in of the MMD Government at the end of October, 1991. There followed a period of uncertainty over the future management of the programme. The steering committee was suspended but the technical committee continued under the oversight of the Ministry of Commerce, Trade and Industry. The new government made a commitment to introduce legislation to facilitate the execution of privatisation.

In July, 1992, the Privatisation Act (No. 21 of 1992) was passed, establishing the Zambia Privatisation Agency (ZPA). The main functions of the Agency were outlined thus:

    (a) Recommend privatisation policy guidelines to Cabinet;

    (b) Implement programme as per approved guideline;

(c) Oversee all aspect of programme;

(d) Monitor progress of programme;

(e) Prepare long-term divestiture plan for approval by Cabinet;

(f) Recommend modes of sale;

(g) Maintain close liaison with relevant institutions;

(h) Publicise activities of the programme.

Clearly, the Act attempted to outline in considerable detail the functions of the Agency to address the many concerns expressed over sound management of this critical programme. The Act went further to spell out the various modes of privatisation the Agency could at its discretion recommend for adoption.

With the establishment of ZPA as a legal entity, the legal institutional basis of Zambia's privatisation programme was now secured. Once in place, the ZPA drew up a divestiture sequence plan which was to be the basis of the execution of the programme. The plan was to span for a period of five to ten years with eleven (11) tranches in all.

The privatisation programme in Zambia has remained active ever since although the momentum has progressively declined with fewer and fewer SOEs still in existence. Considerable progress has been made in advancing the programme, although there are some quarters who feel the programme could go faster. It would be folly to sacrifice thoroughness and transparency in the quest for speed.

Other institutions, complementary to the ZPA, which itself was later absorbed into the Zambia Development Agency (ZDA), have since been established – namely the Lusaka Stock Exchange, now called Lusaka Securities Exchange (LuSE) and the Privatisation Trust Fund. It is expected that in due course, these organs will make their contribution towards attaining some of the goals of the programme, such as broad-based ownership of assets.

THE POST 1991 PERIOD

As seen from the foregoing analysis, the eight years period from 1992 to 2000, was a period of economic transition in Zambia characterised by the process of privatisation of the parastatal sector, as part of the structural economic reforms demanded by the World Bank and the IMF, as a condition for financial support.

During this period, most parastatal companies were privatised, mainly bought by indigenous Zambians under management buyout agreements.

The ZIMCO group was dismantled. Significantly, the mining companies, which were hitherto the backbone of the Zambian economy were sold off to multinational companies most of them at sub-economic prices on the rationale that they were not making profits.

A few of the new investors on the scene turned out to be chancers and of questionable mining experience, and the ventures soon collapsed. Fortunately, some of the new mining investors, such as the VEDANTA Group which came onto the scene in 2003 after the departure of ANGLO, were serious with solid and sustainable investment plans at least during their first years of operations up to 2019 when they fell out with government and were kicked out for alleged incompetence.

These were later joined by other multinationals like GLENCORE, EQUINOX and others which saw the strengthening of the mining industry in private hands, and the consolidation of Corporate Governance Practices.

BACKGROUND TO THE FORMATION OF THE INDUSTRIAL DEVELOPMENT CORPORATION, (IDC)

Since the closure of the Zambia Industrial and Mining Corporation (ZIMCO) Limited and other key corporations such as Industrial Development Corporation (INDECO) and Financial Development Corporation (FINDECO) in the 1990s, SOEs in various sectors had been operating under the direct supervision of line ministries.

It was observed that whereas line ministries were proficient in providing policy guidance, they did not necessarily possess the requisite commercial and investment expertise and resources needed to ensure the positive performance of the SOE under their supervision. As a result, most SOEs were unable to provide Government a return on its investment and contribute to the Treasury by way of dividends.

In addition, the State was unable to maximise the revenue potential of these assets as most of them had not added value to the overall economy and in most cases, had continued to survive on Government direct and indirect subventions. In addition, due to competing demands placed on Government as the shareholder, the SOEs did not benefit from the shareholder in terms of new capital investments. This situation impacted negatively on SOEs in terms of modernisation, growth, governance and accountability.

Until mid-2015, Zambia recorded consecutive positive and increasing GDP growth rates, high foreign direct investment inflows anchored around the resurgence of the mining industry, lower interest rates, reduced volatility in the exchange rates and single digit inflation. In summary, the macroeconomic picture of Zambia had shown tremendous buoyancy and won Zambia acclaim as one of the top ten fastest growing economies in the world between 2011 and 2015.

However, over the same period of high GDP growth rates, formal employment in Zambia recorded minimal increase resulting in the phenomena referred to as "jobless growth."

Unemployment levels remained high and there was a disconnect between low domestic wealth accumulation through job creation and the recorded high economic growth. This posed a serious challenge that called for action and practical strategies and solutions to redress this state of affairs.

The Government, therefore, decided to establish an entity that would serve as a holding company for commercially oriented SOEs, while contributing to accelerating industrialisation, economic diversification, and rural development.

This institution was the Industrial Development Corporation Ltd (IDC).

This move was expected to free the Government to focus on the economy and provide an opportunity for a commercially disciplined and independent company to achieve sustainable returns. In addition to managing its inherited portfolio, such a holding company was expected to actively invest in other local business ventures in Zambia to attain growth and diversification of the economy.

At the time of writing this book, IDC was presiding over a portfolio of about 40 companies in which the state has a stake.

The Industrial Development Corporation (IDC) Limited is a State Owned Enterprise (SOE) charged with the mandate of spearheading the Zambian Government's commercial investments agenda aimed at strengthening Zambia's industrial base and job creation.

The IDC was incorporated in January 2014 and is wholly owned by the Government through the Minister of Finance pursuant to the Minister of Finance (Incorporation) Act Cap 349 of the Laws of Zambia.

The IDC was established to create and maximise long-term shareholder value as an active investor and shareholder of successful state-owned enterprises, as well as undertake industrialisation and rural development activities through the creation of new industries.

The IDC's corporation strategy of 2017 outlines the company's strategic focus during the next five years. It also outlines the role the IDC will play in the industrialisation agenda for the country. Using this plan, the IDC will position itself to be Government's principal special purpose vehicle for industrialisation and investment acceleration.

IDC's *Vision* is to become Africa's performing sovereign Holding Corporation and strategic investment partner. While it's *Mission Statement* is to maximise long-term shareholder value in State-Owned Enterprises and invest in key economic sectors to contribute to industrialisation and sustainable economic growth.

It's *Goal Statement* aims at transforming State-Owned Enterprises towards commercial viability, contribute to industrialisation and job creation.

Governance Structure of the IDC

His Excellency the President of the Republic of Zambia is the Chairperson of the Board. The Board comprises of three (3) Cabinet Ministers-Finance, Commerce Trade and Industry, and Agriculture; two (2) civil servants-the Secretary to the Treasury and Permanent Secretary for Commerce Trade and Industry; seven (7) private sectors members and the Group Chief Executive Officer as an ex-officio member.

IDC Board and Committees

The IDC's Board provides overall guidance and policy directions to its management. The Board meets as required to decide on the following matters:

1. Overall long-term strategic objectives;
2. Major investment and divestment proposals; and
3. Major funding proposals.

To assist the Board in its responsibilities, specific authority is delegated to various Board committees chaired by a non-executive Director who is independent of management.

Investments Committee: Responsible for all investment decisions, including investment policies, investment strategy, and procedures as well as matters pertaining to the effective management and oversight of the IDC's portfolio and subsidiary companies;

Finance and Administration Committee: Responsible for the IDC's Annual Budgets and Work Plans, Financial Management, Staffing and Human Capital Development and ensuring a high-performance work environment is established in the IDC.

Audit and Risk Committee: Responsible for all audit and enterprise risk related matters i.e. internal audit matters as well as statutory audits and risk management pertaining to the IDC as a group including the approval of financial reports.

According to the IDC official documentation, the Strategic objectives of the IDC are spelt out as follows:

1. To reposition all State-Owned Enterprises through improved management, financial viability, and sustainability and bring loss-making entities to profitability;

2. To catalyse private sector investment by co-investing in business venture with the private sector across the forestry, fisheries, agro-processing, renewable energy, mining value addition and tourism sectors;

3. To identify and undertake high risk investments that add value to the country's natural resources;

4. To ensure a balanced and secure return on investment and enhance the capacity of the Corporation to deliver growth to the portfolio;

5. To enhance the legal, institutional and group oversight framework in accordance with the tenets of good corporate governance; and

6. To identify and mitigate risks in the group portfolio and strengthen the credibility and creditworthiness of the Corporation.

(Report of the Committee on Parastatal Bodies 21st September, 2017)

Viewed from the given background and analysis, the incorporation of the IDC represents the PF Government's best option towards improving the corporate governance of SOE's while at the same time providing the best framework of converting its SOE's into productive investments capable of giving Government a reasonable and sustainable return on its investments while at the same time contributing positively to economic growth and job creation.

There are interesting arguments for and against the formation of the IDC. IDC turns six years old in January, 2020.

During the period of its existence economic analysts have pointed out a number of differing observations as to whether the IDC represents a positive development in the economic agenda of the Country or not.

A key and indisputable strength of the establishment of the IDC is that it has stimulated the operational performance of many SOE's which were previously loss making to the extent that some of them have actually started recording profits and declaring dividends to the shareholders. Newspapers regularly carry articles showing the new Chairpersons of the Boards of IDC member Companies handing over handsome cheques in dividends to the Group CEO of IDC, Mateyo Kaluba. Clearly this is a most welcome development as opposed to reading perennial stories about loss making SOE's.

Another notable development has been that the IDC has embraced sound Corporate Governance principles and practices throughout the Group. All IDC Companies are required to formulate strategic plans to guide their operations and in particular, each company is required to sign a Performance Agreement with the IDC as Shareholder. The advantage of this system is that the performance agreement spells out in quantifiable terms the deliverables against which the operating company will be measured in evaluating its performance, at the end of each financial year.

Finally, another upside feature of the IDC is that the Holding Company has succeeded in recapitalising some of its subsidiary companies which hitherto were grossly undercapitalised and consequently could not grow.

On the other side of the argument, economic commentators have observed that the IDC will in the end turn out to be no different from the old ZIMCO, with a huge and costly superstructure with a bloated workforce.

So far the shareholders of the IDC, namely, the Government of the Republic of Zambia, have resisted the temptation to allow the IDC head office to grow into a superstructure with costly overheads. The IDC head office has so far maintained a lean structure, operating as an investment vehicle of government.

One strong criticism, which I have alluded to earlier, is that Corporate Governance practice, does not sit well, when you have the Head of State himself, who is an embodiment of the shareholder chairing the Board of Directors of the IDC.

In Corporate Governance, it is strongly recommended that in a large public organisation such as the IDC the role of the shareholder should be distant and separate from governance. The IDC should be treated like all other state owned enterprises, where the appointment of ministers, and permanent secretaries as board chairperson's was discontinued a long time ago.

The current board composition does not in my view provide the ideal platform for the implementation of unrestrained corporate governance principles and practices.

SUMMARY

This chapter has discussed in-depth the backdrop to Zambia's privatisation policy framework.

The chapter has also given detailed background information to the formation of the Industrial Development Corporation (IDC). At this point, the information presented in this chapter has helped you understand the functions performed by IDC.

CHAPTER 3

THE FIRST STEPS

THE FOUNDING FATHERS AND MOTHERS

The year 2000, will go down in the history of Corporate Governance in Zambia, as one in which the Institute of Directors of Zambia (IoD) was formally established.

The birth of the IoD in Zambia signified the beginning of a spirited campaign to introduce and enhance the practice of sound Corporate Governance principles on the Zambian Corporate landscape.

The credit for initiating the first steps that led to the sowing of the seeds which in turn led to the formation of the IoD in Zambia unquestionably goes to the Association of the Institute of Charted Secretaries and Administrators in Zambia (ICSA Zambia). ICSA Zambia is a Professional Association bringing together professionally qualified Chartered Company Secretaries and Students of the ICSA profession under the aegis of the mother professional body in the United Kingdom. The ICSA has since been branded, The Governance Institute.

HOW IT ALL STARTED

In the cold month of June, 1998, the Institute of Chartered Secretaries and Administrators (Zambia Association) organised a three days' workshop at Intercontinental Hotel in Lusaka, from 22nd to 24th June, 1998 in conjunction with the Commonwealth Programme on Corporate Governance and the Commonwealth Fund for Technical Co-operation. The workshop attracted key stakeholders from across a spectrum of various sectors of the Zambian Society with different professional backgrounds.

Representatives of the Government of the Republic of Zambia, business executives from the private sector, parastatal organisations, diplomatic missions, and the civil society were all present.

Some of the key participants at this ground breaking workshop included; Mr. Michael Gillibrand then Special Adviser – Management and Training Services Division at Commonwealth Secretariat, in London; Mr. Mohan V. Thomas, then reigning Chairman of the Institute of Chartered Secretaries and Administrators (ICSA) in Zambia; Mr. Geoffrey Bowes then Executive Director for the Commonwealth Association for Corporate Governance, New Zealand.

The purpose of this workshop was to formally constitute a team of like-minded people with passion for good Corporate Governance to develop different documents to guide and facilitate the establishment of the Institute of Directors in Zambia. The workshop also intended to provide context to stakeholders as to why establishing the Institute of Directors was relevant and worth undertaking.

The other purpose was to give a complete understanding to the members of the task force of what needed to be accomplished in order to achieve success. The workshop was also used to create mutual understanding among the task force members so as to understand each other's responsibilities. The workshop was used as a platform for illustrating realistic measures of success which were anticipated from the establishment of the IOD.

I am privileged to have participated in this stakeholder meeting in my capacity as Past Chairman of the ICSA, Zambia.

The workshop was officially opened by His Honour the Vice President of the Republic of Zambia, Lt. General Christon Tembo, M.P.

In his speech, the Vice President gave a very clear and unambiguous statement that the Government of Zambia will fully support the growth and development of Corporate Governance in Zambia.

He also made it abundantly clear that going forward, Government would have no business being in business, as it were. The full speech is attached in the appendices section.

The three days' interactive and power point slide presentations, keep in mind that Microsoft PowerPoint slide presentations using projectors with fancy animations sounding like type writers or emergency car breaks had just been introduced in Zambia at that time, was both educative and highly enlightening!

Among the notable presenters who inspired the workshop participants, was a fine gentleman by the name of Boyman Mancama, President of the Institute of Directors of Zimbabwe. The man was so passionate about Corporate Governance not only in Corporate entities but also in Government Institutions. This was the time Robert Gabriel Mugabe, the then President of the Republic of Zimbabwe had just passed a law on Land Reforms in that country and the "Zimbabwean White Farmers" had started trooping away from that country to neighbouring countries including Zambia. The resounding round of applause to Mr. Mancama's presentation was phenomenal.

The full list of Presenters included:

1. **Geoffrey Bowes**
   Chief Executive Officer of the Commonwealth Association for Corporate Governance, New Zealand.

2. **Matthew Durdy**
   Country Director for Commonwealth Development Corporation, Zambia

3. **Michael Gillibrand**
   Special Adviser – Commercialisation in the Commonwealth Secretarial, London U.K

4. M.C.J. Kunkuta

Registrar of Companies, Ministry of Commence, Trade and Industry, Zambia

5. Boyman Mancama

President of the Institute of Directors, Zimbabwe

6. Rodney Rawlinson

Group Company Secretary of Dow Chemicals, South Africa

7. Harriet Sikasote

Lawyer in private practice, Zambia

In terms of the way forward, one fundamental decision that was taken at the conclusion of this ground breaking workshop was a firm resolution to assemble a *"Task Force"* to begin working on the framework and the modalities towards the formation of the Institute of Directors (IoD) in Zambia.

The full list of the names of the people who attended this historic first workshop on Corporate Governance is attached in the appendices section.

The following were appointed by the workshop to constitute this Task Force on 24th June, 1998;

1. Mr. Patrick D. Chisanga   - Chairman
2. Mr. Kenneth Chibesakunda
3. Ms. Joyce Muwo
4. Ms. Mary T. Ncube
5. Mr. Mohan Thomas
6. Mr. Kunda E. Kalaba
7. Mr. Mumba S. Kapumpa
8. Mr. Michael Daka
9. Mr. Stephen Ndhlovu
10. Mr. Charles Mate
11. Mr. Satish Gulati

12. Dr. Herrick Mpuku
13. Mr. Luke Mbewe
14. Mr. Robert Mwambwa
15. Mrs. Elizabeth Jere
16. Mr. Isaac Ponde
17. Mr. Fabiano C. Lukashi (Secretary)

This collection of fine brains and minds was constituted into a Task Force, in June 1998 by the Institute of Chartered Secretaries in Zambia with the specific responsibilities of drawing up a Code of Ethics, Code of Conduct, and the Constitution to form the basis for the establishment of IoD in Zambia, and incorporating the Organisation.

Meetings of the Task Force took place at Zambia Privatisation House (ZPA) now Zambia Development Agency (ZDA) near the New Government Complex House offices. On a bi-weekly basis, meetings would run from 18:30 hours all the way up to and beyond 22:00 hours, depending on the agenda items.. None of the Task force members even attempted to claim or recover their personal costs in drafting the Zambian COE, COC and the Constitution of the IoD. Those days "sitting allowances" in workshops and meetings was the in thing during the Frederick Titus Jacob Chiluba rule as President of the Republic of Zambia. All the members proudly sacrificed their time and personal resources out of commitment to seeing the advancement of Corporate Governance in Zambia.

The Task Force had among other responsibilities, the unenviable task of studying the Codes of Best Practice, the various constitutions which were received from the Institutes of Directors of New Zealand, Zimbabwe and South Africa. Hundreds of hours went into the wading through papers, files, reports, documents and studying of Codes of Conduct, Codes of Ethics, Corporate Governance literature and what it entails. Various research papers and journal publications, constitutions from the Republics of South Africa, Zimbabwe, The United Kingdom, Australia and New Zealand were reviewed.

It was from all these documents that the Task Force ultimately assembled the material to evolve the initial constitutional documents of the IoD of Zambia.

The initial Articles of Association of the IoD Zambia appear in appendices.

In bringing to conclusion, the 18 months long work of the Task Force, and thereby setting the stage for the establishment of IoD Zambia, the Chairman of the Task Force wrote to the secretariat of the Institute of Chartered Secretaries and Administrators requesting for permission to dissolve the Task Force.
After permission was granted the Chairman of the Task Force wrote to each member of the Team, in the following terms, in February 2000;

"We have successfully put together a Constitution for the IoD of Zambia and we have also incorporated it as a company limited by guarantee under the Companies Act. In short, we have delivered our mandate in full, in thanking you for the excellent work done, I think that it is also appropriate that I should announce the formal dissolution of the Task Force. In consequence, I am by copy of this letter advising the Chairman of the ICSA (then Mr. Stephen Ndhlovu), to proceed with the appointment of an interim Board of Directors of the Institute so that it can commence function."

This is the background that set the stage for the eventual establishment of the Institute of Directors of Zambia.

SUMMARY

This chapter has highlighted some major steps which were undertaken by gallant men and women in sowing the seeds which in turn led to the formation of the IoD in Zambia.

The chapter also names the associations, institutions and individuals that played a key role in ensuring that the Institute of Directors was established in Zambia for example the ICSA and many other organisations and individuals as listed earlier.

CHAPTER 4

IoD ZAMBIA IS BORN

THE LAUNCHING OF IoD ZAMBIA

After two years of behind the scenes work by the Task Force, the Institute of Directors of Zambia was officially launched on Friday, 7th April, 2000, by the then Minister of Commerce, Trade and Industry, Mr. William Harrington, MP., at Lusaka's Pamodzi Hotel.

The Official launch of the Institute was coordinated by the Lusaka Securities Exchange stock Exchange in conjunction with the Institute of Chartered Secretaries, Zambia Association and the Commonwealth Association for Corporate Governance.

This ground breaking milestone, was preceded by a half day Corporate Governance Seminar sponsored by the Lusaka Stock Exchange. Notable speakers included Mr. Geoffrey Bowes, CEO Commonwealth Association for Corporate Governance; Mr. Leo Anton Management Consultant from the Ghana State Enterprise Commission; Mr. Mohan Thomas, President of the ICSA Zambia; Mr. Steven Ndhlovu, Interim President of the IoD Zambia and the author of this book, Patrick Chisanga; Mr. Mumba Kapumpa Coordinated the Seminar as Master of Ceremonies.

The official launch culminated into a cocktail party in the evening to celebrate the birth of IoD Zambia.

It was a glorious and sparkling evening which brought together a very large gathering of business executives from all economic sectors with a good blend of the Corporate Governance consultants and practitioners who came from outside Zambia specifically to witness the historic occasion.

Champagne and wine flowed generously as members of the Task Force were being congratulated on a mission accomplished after 18 months of dedicated hard work.

THE INTERIM BOARD OF DIRECTORS

Following the official launch of the IoD Zambia in April, 2000, it became necessary to put together an interim Board of Directors to take over from the Task Force; the responsibility of steering the affairs of the Institute and take matters to the next level.

The responsibility and authority of appointing an interim Board of Directors lay with the Institute of Chartered Secretaries and Administrators in Zambia, who had initiated the whole process of driving the inception of Corporate Governance in Zambia.

Accordingly, in May, 2000, the ICSA appointed an interim Board of Directors.

The IoD Zambia commenced its operations in June, 2000, with the following as the interim board of Directors;

1. Mr. Stephan Ndhlovu — Interim President
2. Mr. Patrick D. Chisanga — Interim Vice President
3. Mr. Esau S. S Nebwe — Interim Director
4. Mr. Fabiano Lukashi — Interim Director
5. Mr. Michael Daka — Interim Director
6. Ms. Mary T. Ncube — Interim Chief Executive

The initial temporary secretariat of IoD Zambia was situated at Plot No. 201, Kasangula road, Roma, Lusaka which was actually the offices of the first Interim Chief Executive Officer Ms. Mary Ncube. After Ms. Mary Ncube, tenure as Interim Chief Executive, another member of the Board, Ms. Joyce Muwo, took over as Executive Director, also serving pro bono from January, 2002 to May, 2003.

IoD Zambia remains eternally indebted to both these ladies for volunteering their services to run affairs of the Institute often at the expense of their own companies.

The initial postal address was Box 50576, Lusaka, the postal address of the Interim Vice President, Mr. Patrick Chisanga's company, Muchanga Investments Limited.

INITIAL WORK PLAN

From the outset, the newly established IoD Zambia presented itself as a leadership forum with a focus on the development of its members through education, information and communication with a view of making positive influence on the entire corporate and public sector environment of Zambia at large. The new institute committed itself to improving and upgrading the corporate governance landscape in Zambia.

As observed earlier, back in 2000, the need for corporate governance in Zambia was very real and imperative. From the back drop of the breakup of parastatal sector in Zambia, and the emergence of a larger private sector, the need for direction, education and training of directors to ensure the highest standards of business ethics and skill and familiarity with the broad functions and fiduciary responsibilities for directors became paramount.

Against this background, IoD Zambia set the following initial objectives which were in line with those of other IoDs in the Commonwealth countries:

1. To promote excellence in Corporate Governance, to represent the interests of directors and facilitate their professional development in support of the economic well-being of the country.

2. To enhance the standards and effectiveness of Directors through information and education on the legal, moral, financial and general rights and responsibilities in respect of their companies, shareholders, employees, management and the community as a whole.

3. To inculcate the highest standards of ethics among directors.

4. To provide an effective voice for company directors in public affairs and for that purpose, take a continuing and effective interest in legislation, economic and social matters and the law generally to ensure the preservation of basic commercial freedom and to prevent abuse of such freedom.

In pursuit of the foregoing objectives, the initial work plan of the IoD Zambia was twofold. The very first task was to launch an aggressive membership drive to attract new members into the institute from both the private and public sector, but with particular focus on the private sector. It was strongly felt that IoD in order to be effective, had to be essentially private sector driven.

The second important task was to develop and initiate a Director Training programme targeted at sitting directors in all companies and organisations. Further discussion on this dimension will follow a little later.

THE FIRST ANNUAL GENERAL MEETING

During our first year in office as interim Board of Directors of the newly formed IoD Zambia, one of our key focus goals was to ensure that as expeditiously as possible, we moved towards convening an AGM with the principal objective of holding elections, to have a democratically elected Board of Directors installed in accordance with the principles of sound Corporate Governance, as was enshrined in the then draft articles of the new Institute.

The challenge we faced in this regard was that the new Institute had absolutely no funds in its coffers. The little money we had raised from early membership fees could not possibly pay for the cost of convening an AGM.

We, therefore, embarked on a spirited fundraising exercise by approaching organisations we believed were keen to support capacity building in corporate governance. We made appointments with the heads of key institutions such as UK's DFID; the USAID; SIDA; UNDP and the EU to mention but a few.

It is noteworthy to record that two of the above institutions, agreed to assist the young IoD Zambia.

The UNDP under the leadership of Mrs. Olubanke King Akerele who was then the Resident Representative of the UNDP in Zambia indicated that while she had no excess funds to donate to the IoD, she offered to provide us with office accommodation rent free in the UN building adjacent to St. Ignatius Catholic Church, in Lusaka. This was a major boost to our operations as an institute because we now had an official office address as IoD, in a centrally located building in the city. This development enabled us to appoint the first full time staff of the IoD, in the name of Mrs. Victoria Silutongwe whom we engaged as the first Administrative Officer, at a modest monthly salary from April, 2003 to July, 2005. Victoria has risen through the IoD ranks progressing from an administrative officer to becoming the Executive Director from August, 2005 to November, 2011. After her retirement as a full time employee in November, 2011, she was appointed as a member of the Corporate Governance Development and Training Committee.

At the 2016 annual general meeting of the Institute, Victoria was elected as the National Vice-President, a position she held until the annual general meeting of March, 2019. At the time of writing Victoria was Acting President and a Fellow of the Institute. As can be seen Victoria has gone through the IoD mill and gained vast experience in corporate governance matters and issues from the numerous trainings and forums attended over the years. During her tenure, she had been instrumental in raising the Institute's profile in advocating for good corporate governance practices in both the private and public sector organisations.

The second important organisation, to whom I would like to record our eternal appreciation, was the Private Sector Development Programme of the EU, (PSDP). Through the assistance of Ms Dora Siliya, who was at that time Executive Assistant to the Director of the PSDP in Zambia, (she later become a Cabinet Minister), she secured an appointment for me to see Mr. Chris Sealy the Director of PSDP, who happens to be an extremely affable gentleman with a positive mindset. Apparently Chris Sealy had been following keenly the unfolding developments leading to the launch of IoD Zambia, in April, 2000. When I tabled our specific request to the effect that the Interim Board was actually seeking financial assistance to enable us convene an AGM to elect a new Board, without any hesitation, Chris Sealy responded that PSDP in fact had a budget to support efforts aimed at capacity building in governance. He advised that we promptly come up with a budget for the AGM to support an appropriate letter of request which we quickly prepared.

Against this background, the Interim Board was enabled to convene our first Annual General Meeting at the Pamodzi Hotel on 31st March, 2001.

The two major items that featured on the Agenda of this first AGM was the adoption of the Articles of Association of the Institute and the election of the Board of Directors.

A copy of the Articles that were adopted at this AGM appears in the appendices.

The following, were elected as the first Board of Directors of IoD Zambia, on 31st March, 2001.

1.	Mr. David A.R. Phiri	President
2.	Mr. Patrick D. Chisanga	Vice President
3.	Ms Mary T. Ncube	Board Member
4.	Mr. Essau Nebwe	Board Member
5.	Mr. Stephen Ndhlovu	Board Member
6.	Miss. Joyce Muwo	Board Member
7.	Mr. Richard Healy	Board Member
8.	Mr. Sebastian Kopulande	Board Member
9.	Mr. Fabiano Lukashi	Board Member

At the conclusion of the elections, the new President of the Institute, Mr. David Phiri, stated that his objective was to help strengthen and consolidate the Institute through his wealth of contacts in the corporate world but that he intended to serve for only one year after which he would want his "younger brother" the Vice President, Patrick Chisanga, to assume leadership of the Institute.

True to his word, Mr. David Phiri served for only one year and at the second AGM. Mr. Phiri did not seek re-election and the Vice President, the author of this book, was elected unopposed as the second President of the Institute of Directors of Zambia.

IoDZ Past And Present Presidents

Mr. Stephan Ndhlovu
Institute of Directors
Interim President

(2000-2001)

Mr. David A.R. Phiri
Institute of Directors
President (2001-2002)

Mr. Patrick D. Chisanga
Institute of Directors
President (2002-2005)

Mr. Esau S.S Nebwe
Institute of Directors

President (2005-2007)

Mr. Mumba Kapumpa, SC
Institute of Directors

President (2007-2010)

Mr. Julu G. Simuule
Institute of Directors

President (2010-2013)

Mrs. Sherry M.A. Thole
Institute of Directors

President (2013-2016)

Prof. Esther M. Nkandu
Institute of Directors

President (2016-2019)

Mrs. Victoria Silutongwe
Institute of Directors

President (2019-.........)

Summary

This chapter has presented a summary of the activities which characterised the glorious and sparkling evening of the launch of the Institute of Directors in Zambia, in April, 2000.

The names of the first elected board of directors of the newly formed Institute of Directors have been revealed. The Initial work plan which was adopted by the board and the date on which the initial AGM was held has also been discussed.

CHAPTER 5

GETTING DOWN TO WORK

From the outset, the freshly elected Board of Directors of the newly launched IoD Zambia, was cognisant of the fact that we needed to hit the ground running, in order not to lose the momentum and enthusiasm that had been generated by the widely publicised launch of the Institute.

The new Board recognised that it was extremely important that the new Institute made impact within the very first few months of coming into office. We, therefore, developed an initial programme of work which included the following key benchmarks:

1. Fundraising
2. Instituting a full time Secretariat
3. Membership Recruitment
4. Director Training
5. Developing the First Code of Best Practice.

In line with the IoD's objectives to promote excellence in corporate governance there was recognition of the need for Director Development through education, training and monitoring to enable our members exercise leadership, enterprise, and integrity to achieve continuing corporate prosperity and to act with best practices.

In order to achieve these objectives, there was need to structure sustainable sources of financing to fund the Institute's broad objectives and activities.

During the IoD's interim stage, the main source of income had been membership contributions. There was a need to further broaden the base of funding in order to generate additional income to finance a much wider spectrum of activities and programmes.

Against this background a broad based fundraising strategy was drawn up, which targeted, membership growth, as well as approaching financial institutions and other co-operating partners for assistance. In this regard approaches were made to the British DFID and Sweden's SIDA, with limited success.

In addition, we launched a programme of hosting fundraising business luncheons, at which we featured a variety of interesting guest speakers from both the public sector and the corporate world; local and international.

Our first goal was membership development both as a way of growing the IoD and a fundraising strategy. Annual membership subscriptions were pegged at K250,000 (un-rebased old currency), as approved at the first AGM.

As at 10th March, 2001, just prior to the first AGM, total membership of the IoD stood at 51. See the full list of members in appendices. This number grew to 73 on the date of the AGM.

In order to boast membership growth, Mr. David Phiri, as President of the IoD, challenged every Board member to strive to bring in at least 5 new members during our first year in office.

This strategy worked well as we began to see a steady growth in membership including corporate membership, during the very first year.

In order to spearhead the activities of the Institute, the Board established seven committees of the Board as follows:

	COMMITTEE	CHAIRPERSON
1.	Membership Development	Sebastian Kopulande
2.	Finance Committee	Mary Ncube
3.	Training and Education	Essau S. Nebwe
4.	Marketing & Promotion	Richard Healey
5.	Membership Services	Joyce Muwo
6.	Government Liaison Committee	Patrick D. Chisanga
7.	Consultancy	Stephen Ndhlovu

IoD Secretariat

Owing to funding limitations, the new IoD Zambia was unable to finance rented office accommodation in its nascent stages, neither were we able to afford to comply full time staff.

One of the Board members Ms. Mary Ncube who had been appointed to serve as Interim CEO of the Institute graciously offered to host the IoD Secretariat at her private office, in Roma, residential area. This was the second time a Board Member housed IoD at their private business premises.

After the first four months, it became clear that the volume of work at the IoD Secretariat was growing rapidly making it difficult for the Interim CEO to cope while running her own business at the same time.

Round about this time, IoD was able to secure some funding from the German Technical Aid to Zambia, GTZ, who agreed to fund the core budget of the IoD Secretariat for 12 months, which included salary for the Executive Secretary plus a variety of office equipment.

Consequently, IoD Zambia was now in a position to open a full time Secretariat with the combined position of Chief Executive and Secretary. Mr. Anthony Matoka was appointed to this full time position.

DIRECTOR TRAINING PROGRAMME

One of the central goals and objectives of setting up the IoD in Zambia was to accelerate Corporate Governance Training for all directors and leaders of corporate entities and organisations in both the public sector and the private sector.

We launched the director training programme in Zambia by first developing a core of trainers who would be formerly schooled in Corporate Governance training.

In order to do this, we sought the support of the Global Corporate Governance Forum (GCGF) of the World Bank, who at that time were running Corporate Governance Trainers Training programmes across the world. With the assistance of the GCGF, IoD Zambia managed to train a large pool of trainers who are now engaged to conduct Director Training programmes on a regular basis.

Director Training now forms a key part of IoD's activities and has grown to become a major source of revenue.

SUMMARY

The interim Board of Directors went down to work immediately after it was inducted. The Board developed an initial programme of work which included the key benchmarks such as fundraising, instituting a full-time secretariat, membership recruitment, director training and developing the first code of best practice.

CHAPTER 6

INTERNATIONAL OUTREACH

In this chapter, I will focus on taking a close look at some of the International Corporate Governance Organisations that have helped to shape the growth and development of corporate governance in Zambia, over the last 20 years.

I have singled out three organisations, all of which I have had the opportunity and privilege to work with, in my various corporate governance capacities over the years. These are:

1. The Commonwealth Association of Corporate Governance, CACG;

2. The Global Corporate Governance Forum, GCGF; and the

3. African Corporate Governance Network, ACGN

THE COMMONWEALTH ASSOCIATION OF CORPORATE GOVERNANCE, CACG

The CACG, was one of the international organisations that played a key role in the formative stages of Corporate Governance in Zambia. I mentioned in Chapter 2 that one of the keynote speakers at the days' inaugural workshop that was organised by the ICSA Zambia, in Lusaka in June, 1998, was Mr. Geoffrey Bowes, who was then serving as Executive Director of the CACG in London.

The history of the birth and development of corporate governance in Zambia would be incomplete, without due recognition of the role that was played by the CACG in the formative years.

It is, therefore, important that I reflect on the origins of the CACG, its structure and the role it played in extending the frontiers of corporate governors in all Commonwealth member countries including Zambia.

The author of this book was privileged to have served on the board of CACG for two years, from 2001 to 2003. Being a member of the Board, as a representative of the IoD Zambia, afforded me a front seat position to observe and participate in delivering the mandate of the CACG.

Background To The Establishment Of The CACG

Whilst issues relating to corporate governance came into the limelight following the spate of corporate collapses in the UK in the mid-1980s, the publication of the Cadbury Report in the UK in 1992 gave it an added dimension. At the same time international interest in corporate governance increased with the financial crises in East Asia in the 1990s. These events drew attention to the vulnerability of cross border investments and the need for more effective governance of corporations, whether in the public or the private sector. This led to a number of world-wide initiatives for promoting corporate governance. Global standards of corporate governance are now recognised as a crucial part of the global financial architecture.

However, the particular interest in corporate governance in the Commonwealth emerging markets had its origins not so much in the context of the private sector financial systems as in the need to improve the performance and then to privatise state enterprises. The weaknesses of state enterprise boards, the issues of the accountability of the chief executive and the management team to the board and to their supervising ministry, the strategic effectiveness and the operational efficiency of state enterprises had long been matters of concern in the Commonwealth.

After 1992, many member countries including Zambia experienced an increase in the privatisation of state enterprises, and consequently suffered from a 'post-privatisation policy vacuum.' This meant that the policy and the institutional environment were inadequate to cope with the demands of privatisation. Whilst the Commonwealth recognised, monitored and evaluated this lack of essential institutional fabric to sustain fair competition and appropriate regulation through its regular policy workshops, its view was that the scale of agenda required to deal with this policy vacuum was enormous, and the time required for implementing appropriate polices was extensive. Hence, it concentrated on a few powerful instruments, which had significant short-term impact. This focus, according to the Commonwealth, was not to be at the expense of longer-term actions necessary to build the essential elements of an effective regulatory environment, but that it was to be earliest phase of the longer and wider process of reform and capacity building for the 'post-privatisation environment.'

Accordingly, the Commonwealth identified corporate governance as an important policy instrument requiring its technical assistance. Although corporate governance was not to be seen as some sort of panacea, nevertheless, the Commonwealth believed that the widespread practice of good corporate governance would help to achieve multiple objectives in emerging markets.

The other reason given by the Commonwealth for concentrating on corporate governance as a policy instrument was the relative ease with which capacities would be developed through institution building and training. It described this as a 'critical mass' that could be established, for example, by working through IoDs and Institutes of Chartered Secretaries.

The Commonwealth approach to corporate governance was an attempt to achieve the optimum combination of the fundamental imperatives of performance, conformance and consensus in the specific circumstances of a particular country. Therefore, the Commonwealth recognised corporate governance as the means, by which among other, would contribute to:

1. Increased probity, efficiency and effectiveness of the financial markets, which in turn increased direct and portfolio investor confidence to commit long term funds to the country;

2. Improved operational and strategic competitiveness of Commonwealth enterprises operating in the global market;

3. The self-regulation of corporations, especially newly privatised utilities and public service enterprises, thereby, facilitating more effective privatisation.

For these reasons, corporate governance was perceived as a powerful 'lever' for change, and included as a high priority item on the agenda. Thus, at the Commonwealth Business Forum in 1997, the recommendation was made that:

"Capacity should be established in all Commonwealth countries to create or reinforce institutions to promote good corporate governance: in particular, codes of good practice establishing standards of behaviour in the public and private sector should be agreed to secure greater transparency and to reduce corruption."

This resolution was endorsed in the Commonwealth Heads of Government Edinburgh Economic Declaration in October, 1997.

Against this background, the Commonwealth Association for Corporate Governance (CACG) was established in April, 1998, in response to the Edinburgh Declaration. Its membership was drawn from various organisations, institutions and individuals within the Commonwealth. Core members included the Institute of Directors (IoDs) in member countries, branches of the Institute of Chartered Secretaries (ICSAs), and special interest groups of professional associations of accountancy, law, banking etc.

The CACG saw itself as a focal point for promoting corporate governance systems and encouraged national professional institutes in member countries to become part of this global network of international professional institutes. It had a five-year target in which it hoped to establish, through these professional institutes, self-sustaining institutional capacities for corporate governance to cover each of the Commonwealth emerging markets, developing countries and associate states. The aim was to promote and safeguard widespread practice of the highest standards of business direction in the private and public sectors.

The CACG received financial support from the Commonwealth Secretariat, the World Bank, the Government of New Zealand, and Commonwealth Fund for Technical Co-operation (CFTC) and other international Agencies.

OBJECTIVES OF THE COMMONWEALTH ASSOCIATION FOR CORPORATE GOVERNANCE (CACG)

The main objectives of the CACG were:

1. To promote good standards of corporate governance and business practices in the public and private sectors of the Commonwealth as a means to achieve global standards of efficiency, commercial probity and effectiveness in economic and social development;

2. To facilitate the development of appropriate institutions that will advance, teach and disseminate such standards; and

3. To strengthen the capacities of all member countries to maintain and extend good practice in corporate governance.

In implementing corporate governance strategies in the Commonwealth, the CACG designed a comprehensive package of activities, which acted as a platform that, ensured the process not only conformed with standards of international best practice, but also, directly linked to national priorities and concerns. These activities included:

National 'road shows' comprising a three days' policy workshops which launched the programme in each country, introduced the debate on the issues and dimensions of corporate governance and included;

1. Short training courses for company chairpersons, non-executive directors, chief executives and company secretaries;

2. Formation of a task forces to take on the responsibility of leading the national programme;

3. Providing assistance with the preparation of a national strategy for the promotion of corporate governance, in co-ordination with other key policy issues and national priorities in the country;

4. Assisting with the drafting of customised national guidelines for corporate governance, adapted from the generic CACG Guidelines "Principles of Corporate Governance in the Commonwealth;"

5. The establishment, or strengthening of professional institutions responsible for promoting corporate governance in the country or region;

6. Follow up training courses for company chairpersons, company directors, corporate secretaries and other officers of enterprises engaged in the corporate governance framework at regional and national level.

CACG GUIDELINES

In addition to the activities for promoting corporate governance, the CACG also issued guidelines. The development of the CACG Guidelines, "Principles of Corporate Governance in the Commonwealth," and its adoption in 1999 constituted an important aspect of the Commonwealth corporate governance initiatives. These guidelines were intended to facilitate best business practice and behaviour, whether in the private or the public sector.

They were neither mandatory nor prescriptive, and had been designed to be evolutionary in concept in order to be able to respond to further developments in corporate governance in the global arena.

The CACG guidelines comprised of 15 principles of corporate governance which had been structured to accommodate the needs of emerging and transitional economies, which made up a large part of the Commonwealth, as well as the more advanced economies and their international investors.

The guidelines were aimed primarily at boards of directors with a unitary board structure, most common in Commonwealth countries.
Thus they applied to boards of directors, executive and non-executive of all forms of business enterprises, including non-governmental organisations and agencies.

ACHIEVEMENTS OF THE CACG

The efforts of the CACG in promoting good corporate governance in both the public and the private sectors in the Commonwealth are commendable. The initiatives, which commenced in 1996, have since extended to many emerging economies within the Commonwealth, including Botswana, the Caribbean, Kenya, Tanzania, Uganda, Rwanda, Fiji, Gambia, Ghana, India, Malawi, Mauritius, Mozambique, Papua New Guinea, Sierra Leone, Sri Lanka, India and Zambia.

In 2000, the Commonwealth introduced a significant new initiative, which focused on the banking sector, working through the various Central Banks. The following were the reasons advanced for this special focus:

(a) The banking sector is absolutely critical, and can be likened to the bloodstream of the economy – if the banking sector is healthy the rest of the economy can be strong; if the banking sector is poisoned by poor corporate governance the whole economy will be infected, which can lead to collapse;

(b) In many developing countries the equity markets are small and do not play a strong role in the national capital markets, as many companies rely more on debt finance from their banks; in this context there are no institutional investors to perform the powerful role to encourage corporate governance as in OECD countries, but this function can be fulfilled to some extent by the banks;

(c) Central Banks can exert moral suasion and influence over the commercial banks and set requirements for all licensed commercial banks in accordance with the standards set by the Bank for International Settlements; the commercial banks can in turn recommend good corporate governance practices for their corporate customers (including majority of the private and family owned companies which are not publicly listed and subject to the stock exchange) in order to reduce their risk.

Lastly, the Commonwealth was aware that if its corporate governance initiatives were to succeed, the issue of corruption could not be overlooked. Corruption can take many forms and occurs within the public and the private sectors, and not necessarily associated with any particular type of political/ social system, form of government, or level of economic development. Bad governance and corruption are hindrances to economic development. Accordingly, the Commonwealth is aware of this and set itself to tackle the problem head-on. All Commonwealth countries which had not already done so were required to develop and implement their own national good government and anti-corruption strategies.

PROGRAMME OF ACTION OF THE CACG

The CACG had set out an agenda which concentrated in five main areas:

1. Extension of the national 'road shows' to those regions which had not yet been fully covered; the Caribbean, parts of Central Asia and the Pacific;

2. Expansion of corporate governance practice to new areas, such as banking, co-operatives and public sector bodies;

3. An intensive training programme, developed through regional centres of excellence in director training, and the training of trainers in courses at the established institutes, in this area a new initiative had been launched in mid-2001, to train a 'critical mass' of directors in member countries on a 40-hour intensive training course in corporate governance for company directors; this course was comprehensive, examined and certified by the CACG. It involved not only knowledge and skills training but practical assignments to plan specific changes in the participants' own companies and changes to their annual reports, and was designed to both upgrade the proficiency of directors and signal the markets, stakeholders and governments that the corporate sector was making a serious investment in improved corporate governance;

4. Technical support for the newly established institutions to assist them in becoming self-sustaining;

5. Contribution to the international debate on corporate governance through the Global Corporate Governance Forum, and through the Commonwealth structures of the Business Forum and ministerial meetings.

Furthermore, the CACG had longer-term objectives for its national workshops and follow up programmes, which were intended to work towards:

i)   Improving the strategic direction of state enterprises by providing appropriate training for the top executives in these countries to make them compete effectively in the global market;

ii) Granting international recognition to countries which had in place good corporate governance standards as priority locations for investment;

iii) Ensuring high standards of corporate citizenship and business ethics among national companies and foreign direct investors in all participating countries;

iv) Establishing self-sustaining national institutes that could maintain and promise best practice in corporate governance for the benefit of their countries, adequately supported through a network of international Commonwealth connections.

The Commonwealth believed that these initiatives in the long-term will contribute to the ultimate economic and social goals of increased competitiveness and greater public responsibility of the national corporate entities, with consequent increased employment, wage levels, trade, investment and creation of wealth in the participant countries. Although aware that complications may arise in the implementation of some of these initiatives, the Commonwealth was assured that a combination of factors including, the network of relationships and on-going training as well as the fact that the corporate governance model being advocated for had been tried and tested, will act as drivers, which will ensure their implementation.

Viewed in historical perspective today, there can be no doubt that the CACG formed one of the solid pillars which has anchored the development of corporate governance in emerging member countries including Zambia, over the last 30 odd years.

THE CENTER FOR INTERNATIONAL PRIVATE ENTERPRISE

The Center for International Private Enterprise (CIPE) is a non-profit, private sector organisation that provides financial support in the form of grants to non-government business organisations such as chambers of commerce, employers' federations, trade associations, and private enterprise-oriented research groups throughout the world.

CIPE's overall purpose is to encourage the growth of private enterprise principles and organisations that contribute to democratic development.
In 2006 CIPE identified IoD and funded the project "Promoting Corporate Governance in Zambia." The period of support was from 1 August, 2006 to 31 July, 2007.
The project objectives were:

i) To strengthen corporate governance in the SME sector to ensure sustainable growth of the sector whose aim was to ascertain corporate governance practices in selected firms and companies.

ii) To develop a corporate governance code for SMEs

iii) To educate the key decision makers in government on what corporate governance is through one-day seminars for permanent secretaries and members of parliament. The seminars highlighted the key elements in corporate governance and why it is important to the economy of Zambia.

iv) To educate the public, using mass media as an outreach tool, on corporate governance so that the public can hold public officials and private corporations accountable. This included weekly radio programmes on Radio Phoenix for an eight weeks' period and on television with the Zambia National Broadcasting Corporation for a six weeks' period. In addition, IoD published ten articles on corporate governance in the Business Post Newspaper.

The Global Corporate Governance Forum, GCGF

The Global Corporation Governance Forum is a multi-donor trust fund which was founded in 1999 by the World Bank Group and the Organisation for Economic Co-operation and Development (OECD) to promote global, regional and local initiatives that aim at improving the institutional framework and practices of corporate governance. The Forum contributes to the efforts of the international community to promote the private sector as an engine of growth, reduce the vulnerability of developing and transition economies to financial crises, and provide incentives for corporations to invest and perform efficiently, in a socially responsible manner. The Forum seeks to address corporate governance weaknesses of middle income and low income countries in the context of broader national or regional economic reform programmes, which it seeks to complement and enhance. Thus the Forum's activities promote sustainable economic growth and poverty reduction within the framework of agreed international development targets.

HIGHLIGHTS

Over the last 20 years, the Global Corporate Governance Forum (the Forum) has developed an extensive work programme to support corporate governance reform in developing countries. Some highlights from the first phase of the Forum's work programme include the following:

Raising Awareness and Building Consensus

The Forum has supported public-private dialogue in every region, leading to a series of regional policy papers. Roundtables in Asia, Eurasia, Latin America, Russia, and South Eastern Europe have been led by the OECD, in partnership with the World Bank Group and local groups. Forums in Africa, the Caribbean, and the Middle East and North Africa have been organised with support from the Center for International Private Enterprise and the Commonwealth Secretariat.

Building Capacity

Through residential Train the Trainers programmes held in cooperation with the International Institute for Corporate Governance at Yale University, the Forum has supported regional director training networks as they develop local case studies and training curricula. Corporate governance reform leaders in East Asia and Latin America have participated in residential summer programmes.

Sponsoring Research

To support the corporate governance policy agenda with substantive evidence and data, the forum has launched a Global Corporate Governance Research Network convened by Stijn Claessens and Florencio Lopez de Silanes. The network has reviewed the literature on corporate governance and development and identified priorities for further research.

Disseminating Best Practice

The Forum supports networks that exchange and disseminate information about effective reform strategies and techniques through toolkits and case studies. The first toolkit developed by the Forum dispenses practical experience from corporate directors in sound corporate governance practices.

THE PRIVATE SECTOR ADVISORY GROUP OF THE GCGF

In December 2002, soon after I had been elected President of the IoD Zambia, I was appointed to serve as a member of the Private Sector Advisory Group, PSAG, which had been created by the Global Governance Forum.

My appointment was at the invitation of my old friend Phil Armstrong who had at that time been recently appointed as Head of the Global Corporate Governance Forum, a division of the IFC under the World Bank Group in Washington, DC.

The PSAG, brought together 65 international business leaders of the private sector, from across the world, whose shared goal was to help developing Countries improve their Corporate Governance practices.

The PSAG Group included three people from the continent of Africa, namely, Prof. Mervyn King SC and Mr. Roel Khoza both from South Africa and Mr. Patrick D. Chisanga, from Zambia (author of this book).

Through the PSAG, the IFC has been able to bring the practical experience of the international private sector to bear upon the issues and challenges facing corporate governance in developing countries.

PSAG members participate in many IFC activities across the globe, providing counsel and new strategies and sharing their practical experience with the Forum's global networks. PSAG members' efforts include involvement in IFC international consultations, publications, practical guides and capacity building programmes.

It was in my capacity as a PSAG member that I was assigned to help launch the Institute of Directors in Malawi in June, 2010, in Mozambique in 2012, as well as in Namibia in March, 2018.

ACHIEVEMENTS OF THE GCGF

In reviewing the first phase of the work of the GCGF, Anne Simpson, who served as the first Manager of the Forum, made the following reflections.

"The Forum has made great progress in meeting its first objective-to raise awareness and build consensus. The work has been given momentum by recent corporate scandals, which fostered worldwide concern with corporate governance in developed and developing markets.

Corporate governance has been in the headlines in many parts of the world, and it is the head of the policy agenda in many developed as well as developing countries.

Building on this high level of interest worldwide, the Forum has sponsored Round-tables and forums in each region with the aim of building coalitions for reform, around an agenda that identifies common objectives and a shared approach to problem solving. The aim has been to develop networks engaged with reform and develop strategies which reflect local priorities. Participants from over 80 developing countries, from over 500 public and private sector organisations, have taken part in Forum sponsored policy dialogue.

To promote regional dialogue on corporate governance, the Forum has supported the World Bank Group-OECD Roundtables, which have promoted public-private dialogue within the frame of the OECD Principles of Corporate Governance. These Principles have been adopted by the Financial

Stability Forum as one of the 12 standards and codes that underpin the international financial architecture. The regional Roundtables have been an important mechanism for introducing the principles to developing countries. Roundtables in Asia, Eurasia, Latin America, Russia and South Eastern Europe are now producing their strategies for implementing reform through a series of White Papers and Issue Papers.

To ensure regional balance and meet the needs of both low and middle income countries, the Forum has also provided core funding and organisational support to the development of parallel initiatives to promote policy dialogue on corporate governance: the Pan African Consultative Forum; a series of country workshops in the Middle East and North Africa, and the Caribbean Corporate Governance Forum. The Forum has partnered with other international groups in these regions, such as the Commonwealth and the Center for International Private Enterprise.Throughout the Forum's first phase, the International Finance Corporation has provided key support to development and delivery of the work programme.

As the process of policy dialogue has unfolded, many meetings have high-lighted the need to train directors. Most regions have identified a severe constraint on their progress: a shortage of independent and qualified directors to serve on the boards of companies, and ensure that corporate governance reforms are put into practice where it matters-at the company level. To begin to address the need, the Forum has piloted two regional train the trainers programmes-for East Asia and Latin America-which provide training organisations with support for curriculum and case study development.

Linked to this, the Forum has developed a toolkit on institution building, to distil practical step-by-step advice on setting up a sustainable organisation that trains directors. The aim is to support independent organisations that can train directions, develop codes of conduct, and act as advocates for good practice in developing countries.

In many regions, the next stage will be to focus upon implementation as the reform cycle moves beyond awareness raising and consensus building. There is a contributing need to support capacity building and maintain the exchange of best practices through the global network that the Forum has established with its partners in every region. The Forum's commitment to public-private partnership will continue"

Clearly, the GFCG has played an important catalytic role in stimulating and extending the frontiers of Corporate Governance in emerging economies including Zambia. The current Training of Trainers course which has been sustained by IoD Zambia for instance, was initiated by the GFCG who actually conducted the first Training of Trainers programme in Zambia and supplied both the resource persons needed as well as the necessary funding.

There is all the evidence that Zambia and other Countries in Africa, have been big beneficiaries of the GCGF.

THE AFRICAN CORPORATE GOVERNANCE NETWORK, ACGN
The ACGN was formed in 2013 to develop the institutional capacity of ACGN members for enhancing effective corporate governance practices towards building better private and public sector organisations and corporate citizens in Africa.

HISTORY AND BACKGROUND
The Mauritius Institute of Directors (MIoD) together with the Institute of Directors South Africa (IoDSA) jointly spearheaded the settling up of the ACGN, with the support of the NEPAD Business Foundation. The ACGN founding meeting was held in Johannesburg in January, 2013, with a follow-up meeting being held in Harare in June, 2013, with representatives of similar institutions from the following countries: Kenya, Malawi, Morocco, Mozambique, Nigeria, Senegal, Tanzania, Uganda, Zambia and Zimbabwe,

along with MIoD and IoDSA – a total of 12 countries/organisations. Collaborations present at the meetings included World Bank, IFC, Standard Bank, ACCA, Ernst & Young and NEPAD Business Foundation (who currently act as Secretariat of the ACGN on pro bono basis).

At the meeting held in Harare in June, 2013, the Mission, Vision, Values and Objectives were approved, together with the ACGN logo. A Constitution and an Operating Plan were tabled for discussion and the Action Plan was updated. A SWOT analysis was also undertaken and key focus areas were identified and agreed upon.

Under the sponsorship of the IFC, a member of the World Bank Group, the African Corporate Governance Network, held its first Executive Committee meeting on 16th October, 2013 in Mauritius. The ACGN elected Mrs. Jane Valls, CEO of the MIoD, and Mr. Said Kambi, CEO of the Institute of Directors Tanzania, as its first Chairman and Deputy whereby all ACGN Founding Members and the NEPAD Business Foundation signed the ACGN Constitution, which would bind them to work together to promote good corporate governance in Africa.

IoD Zambia was represented by Prof. Esther Munalula Nkandu then Chair of the IoD Board Training Committee, Mrs. Sabina Luputa, then Executive Director of IoD Zambia and Patrick Chisanga as Past President of IoD Zambia.

There is little doubt that the ACGN has achieved the stature of being Africa's umbrella authority on Corporate Governance. It continues to attract the active participation of all existing and emerging Institutes of Corporate Governance on the Continent. The newest member being the Institute of Corporate Governance of Namibia which was launched in Windhoek in March, 2018.

The current membership of the ACGN includes 19 Institutes of Corporate Governance drawn from the following countries:
Algeria, Egypt, Ethiopia, Ghana, Ivory Coast, Kenya, Malawi, Mauritius, Morocco, Mozambique, Namibia, Nigeria, Senegal, South Africa, Tanzania,

Tunisia, Uganda, Zambia and Zimbabwe.

Clearly, the ACGN is set to continue to grow from strength to strength, going forward.

VISION:

ACGN assigned itself the following vision:

"Africa, a continent committed to effective corporate governance and ethical leadership."

VALUES

The Continental Forum adopted the following values from inception.

1. *Transparency* – Being open and clear
2. *Integrity* – Ethical behaviour and consistency of actions and values
3. *Teamwork and Collaboration* – leveraging collective knowledge
4. *Accountability* – Being answerable to stakeholders
5. *Diversity* – Being respectful of the diversity of the African continent

OBJECTIVES

The following were the initial objectives that the ACGN set for itself:

1. Exchange and share knowledge, information, best practices tools and resources.
2. Demonstrating good practice within member organisations and network
3. Building sustainable capacity to enable membership organisations to achieve their goals
4. Common platform for advocacy, initiatives and communications
5 Expand the network
6. Create a favourable climate
7. Conduct research

SUMMARY

This chapter took a close look at some of the international corporate governance organisations that have helped shape the development of corporate governance in Zambia.

The organisations that gave it all to see corporate governance develop in Zambia are many but this chapter has singled out the following for their key roles that they played;

1.   The Commonwealth Association of Corporate Governance, (CACG)
2.   The Global Corporate Governance Forum of the World bank (GCGF)
3.   The African Corporate Governance Network (ACGN)

CHAPTER 7

THE IMPACT OF CORPORATE GOVERNANCE ON NATIONAL ECONOMIC DEVELOPMENT

I have a view that Africa stands on the threshold of a major corporate governance transformation across the continent. More and more governments on the continent of Africa, are in varying degrees beginning to accelerate the implementation of corporate governance reforms in their economies.

It was for example, extremely delightful to listen to the speech of the new President of South Africa Mr. Cyril Ramaphosa, during his very first State of the Nation address to the first sitting of the Parliament of South Africa, in February, 2018, when he said;

"The Government would urgently overhaul the appointment of oversight boards of State Owned Enterprises (SOEs), which up to now had been plagued by allegations of corruption financial mismanagement and maladministration."

Quite clearly, there is a strong wind of corporate governance reform blowing across Africa. This is indeed a most welcome development going forward.

Back home former International Monitory Fund Communication Advisor Mr. Chibamba Kanyama in 2017 during the Good Governance Workshop organised by the Institute of Directors Zambia observed that the future seem to be bright in Corporate Governance in the country with the establishment of Industrial Development Corporation to regulate government run institutions. He pointed out that poor corporate governance, uncertainty in tenure of office by institution's Chief Executives and lack of ethical leadership in the past led to the collapse of several institutions in the country.

I should caution however, that Corporate Governance is not an overnight wonder. It is a journey and, sometimes, a slow journey which will present many challenges as well as opportunities. Corporate Governance is not necessarily about compliance to a set of rules and regulations alone. It should, preferably, be about putting in place better informed boards and improving the quality of corporate and management performance, in all our economic organisations and other institutions.

Corporate Governance is not about quick fixes, but a methodical and patient process that must be relevant and appropriate to each country's stage of development.

In my own country, Zambia, for instance, we launched IoD Zambia 19 years ago, in July, 2000, with the assistance of the Commonwealth Association for Corporate Governance. It took us over two years to get IoD Zambia to be fully established and to become financially independent. Over the last 18 years we have managed to develop a strong and sustainable director training programme which now embraces the public sector, the Corporate world, NGO's and SME's.

IoD has managed to train over 2,000 directors across sectors and, thereby, contributing significantly to improved boardroom performance, in various companies and organisations in our country. Director training has been given top priority in Zambia, in the last 15 odd years, because it has been appreciated that good Corporate Governance starts with individual directors in the boardroom.

Bob Garratt, one of Britain's eminent authorities on Corporate Governance, emphasises the importance of well-trained directors, in his book *"The Fish Rots From the Head."* It is precisely in order to ensure that the "head" does not rot, that we have embarked upon a relentless and sustained corporate governance training program in all our corporate entities. As a result, we have witnessed over the last 15 years, economic vibrancy unfolding in our corporate entities in Zambia, across sectors.

It is an undeniable fact that the sound corporate governance will lead to better companies and stronger economies. It is against this background, that I would like to reflect on the role and the impact of Corporate Governance on sustainable development in emerging economies such as the African economies.

During his state visit to Ghana, in July, 2009, the First Black President of the United States of America, Barrack Obama, had the following to say on the issue of development in Africa.

"Africa's future is up to Africans. Development depends upon good governance. That is the ingredient which has been missing... That is the change that can unlock Africa's potential....it is a responsibility that can only be met by Africans."

These words ring true for each and every country on the African continent. In this chapter, I will attempt to build upon these famous and important words as a foundation for my reflections on the imperative for sound corporate governance practices in Africa economies.

For a long time, Africa in general, apart from South Africa, perhaps, is a continent that has historically attracted very little investment, over the years. Fortunately, this trend is now beginning to change and quite clearly, the emergence of sound corporate governance principles and practices has had a very significant impact. It is to be hoped that improved corporate governance, especially when conducted in the context of wider economic and systemic governance, will enhance investor confidence both domestic and foreign.

I will focus specifically on the SADC region, which embraces 15 countries in the lower part of sub Saharan Africa. The SADC region includes, in alphabetical order; Angola; Botswana; Congo DR; Lesotho; Madagascar; Malawi; Mauritius; Mozambique; Namibia; Seychelles; South Africa; Swaziland; Tanzania; Zambia and Zimbabwe.

The Global Corporate Governance Forum of the World Bank states in its mission statement, that, *"Corporate Governance has become an issue of worldwide importance. The corporation has a vital role to play in promoting economic development and social progress. It is the engine of growth internationally and increasingly responsible for providing employment, goods and services both in the public and private sectors, as well as the development of infrastructure. The efficiency and accountability of the corporation is now a matter of both private and public interest, and governance has, thereby, risen to the top of the international agenda."*

This exemplifies the now indisputable position that Corporate Governance has assumed in the economic development of nations of the world, with particular significance for the emerging and developing economies of the third world in general and our region in particular.

Good Corporate Governance has become imperative as a beacon to attract investors - both local and foreign – and assure them that their investments will be secure and efficiently managed in a transparent and accountable process. Corporate Governance has become a necessary lever in creating competitive and efficient companies and business enterprises and in enhancing the accountability and performance of those entrusted to manage corporations.

Without efficient companies or business enterprises, our countries in the SADC region will not create wealth or employment. Without new investments our companies will stagnate and collapse. And if business enterprises in Namibia, Mozambique, Zambia, Malawi, Angola, Swaziland and in the entire region do not prosper; there will be no economic growth, no employment, no taxes paid and, invariably, the countries of our region will not develop to the best of their potentialities.

Looking at our region, through the lenses of SADC, we can see that the SADC vision is one of a common future, a belief in a regional community that will ensure economic wellbeing; improvement of the standards of living and quality of life; freedom and social justice, peace and security for the peoples of southern Africa. This shared vision is anchored on the common values and principles as well as the historical and cultural affinities that exist between the peoples of southern Africa. Some of the objectives of SADC as stated in article 5 of the SADC treaty are as follows:

- To achieve economic development and economic growth, alleviate poverty, enhance the standard and quality of life of the people of southern Africa and support the socially disadvantaged, through regional integration.
- SADC also seeks to promote self-sustaining development on the basis of collective self-reliance and the interdependence of member states.

Quite evidently, the goals of SADC and the objectives of corporate governance, sound all too clearly, like two sides of the same coin. The two, therefore, possess a common destiny with common ideals.

When we examine the current status of corporate governance in the 15 countries in southern Africa that make up the SADC region, we observe that there are some sharp disparities between the levels of economic development attained and the levels of new investments flowing into the various countries of the region.

It is also curious to observe that there are also significant disparities in the achieved levels of corporate governance amongst different SADC member countries.

Interestingly, countries that have attained higher levels of corporate governance reform such as South Africa, Zambia, Mauritius, Seychelles, Botswana, Mozambique and, recently Namibia, are also exhibiting growing levels of investor confidence and economic growth.

Another pertinent and relevant observation in this regard, are the findings of the now widely acclaimed Ibrahim Index of African governance, managed by the Mo Ibrahim Foundation, which seeks to evaluate the levels of good governance in 48 sub Saharan countries using 5 governance categories, namely:

1. Sustainable economic opportunity;
2. Human development;
3. Safety and security;
4 Rule of law, transparency and corruption; and
5. Participation and human rights.

Once again, it is interesting to observe that the Mo Ibrahim Index has continued to rank Mauritius, Seychelles, Botswana, South Africa, Namibia, Malawi, Madagascar and Zambia among the top 20 countries. This is a very similar profile to that observed with regard to the level of development of Corporate Governance, in the region.

To my mind, there can be little doubt that there is a very strong correlation between good public governance, good Corporate Governance and the levels of economic advancement achieved by the countries of our region.

Zambia presents a good example of the impact of sound Corporate Governance as a driver for sustainable economic development. Over the last 15 odd years, the Zambian economy has experienced phenomenal economic growth on the back of increased investor confidence.

According to ZDA published figures, during the period 2000 to 2015, Zambia recorded an increase in Foreign Direct Investment from around US$ 400,000 in 2005 to approximately US$ 4billion in 2015 across sectors. The Zambian economy also experienced remarkable macroeconomic stability during the same period with interest rates and annualised inflation recording single digit figures. In addition the economy also reflected an average GDP growth rate of around 6.5% over the same period.
(Zambia Development Agency Publication, 2017)

The interesting point to observe is that, this period also coincided with the period that saw accelerated Corporate Governance reform, in the country. Surely, these economic gains were no accidental. The increased confidence in Zambia is quite clearly attributable to the political stability exhibited in the country as much as to the enhanced levels of Corporate Governance practices.

Given this analysis, what then should be the way forward for our region?
It is my view that economic integration in the SADC region will remain lopsided for as long as there exist vast imbalances in the economic development patterns of the member countries. There will be need to level the playing field, as it were. It is also my view that corporate governance can be used as an effective tool in bringing about a level economic playing field in our region by making each country an attractive investment prospect.

As a region, therefore, our governments should be concerned with the need to establish appropriate legal, economic and institutional environments, that will facilitate and allow business enterprises to grow, thrive and prosper as institutions for maximising shareholder value, while, at the same time, being conscious of providing for the wellbeing of all other stakeholders and society as a whole.

Our governments should take deliberate measures to put in place and maintain enabling environments in which efficient and well managed companies can thrive.

The role of the Institutes of Directors in this regard is to promote high standards of corporate governance in both the private and public sectors, through education, training, and participation at relevant fora, thus, ensuring the highest professional and ethical standards amongst directors and the boards on which the directors serve.

As one of the founding fathers of the Institute of Directors of Zambia, I can state with a degree of pride and satisfaction that the advancement of sound corporate governance practices in Zambia, has played a key and significant role in the economic development of Zambia over the last 20 or so years.

Formal director training was instituted by the IoD targeted at directors of boards in both the State Owned Enterprise (SOE) as well as private companies and organisations including family held companies.

Both public and private companies in Zambia are increasingly becoming compliant with sound principles of corporate governance. For example, now companies hold board meetings on regular basis in order to ensure that the directors keep abreast of any issues that are facing the business and are able to pass resolutions concerning its management. Boards are clearly taking control of the running of their companies.

Office holders are appointed transparently, for instance, board of directors vote to elect chairpersons from amongst themselves. Company secretaries are appointed to ensure that board and general meetings are properly convened, that relevant information is distributed, and that accurate minutes are kept.

Annual general meetings of the shareholders are held within the stipulated periods at the end of each of financial year. Companies are now able to maintain physical and electronic copies of important corporate governance documents such as financial statements, minutes of board and general meetings, contracts entered into by the company and correspondence with the public authorities for the periods of upto 7 years.

In addition to that, Zambian companies are becoming more and more tax compliant, thereby generating the much needed tax revenue that the government needs. Companies that were once loss making machines are now declaring handsome profits. Examples include, Kagem, ZANACO, and ZCCM-IH to name a few SOE's. In the process, several corporate governance consulting firms have come to the fore, working hand in hand with the IoD in director training, as well as developing corporate governance instruments and systems in companies and organisations both in the public sector as well as the private sector.

Board Charters and Codes of Corporate Governance are progressively being developed. The Lusaka Securities Exchange for instance (LuSE), has since instituted a code of Corporate Governance for listed companies.

The Financial Sector Development Programme was also instituted under the aegis of the Bank of Zambia. Boards of Directors are beginning to assume their rightful authority and accountability over their companies. GRZ is beginning to understand and appreciate its role as a shareholder.

To further strengthen good corporate governance in the financial sector in Zambia, amendments have been done to the Banking and Financial Services Act on the need for majority non-executive directors on boards, screening of shareholders, CEO and CFO by the Bank of Zambia and the cap of 25% shareholding in financial institutions.

Bank of Zambia has developed a code of good corporate governance for all the financial market licensees and participants, which have prescribed the best practice principles to be followed. Bank of Zambia has also facilitated the adoption of good corporate governance principles by encouraging institutional investors to invest only in companies that observe good corporate governance structures. The enactment of the new Companies Act has also helped in strengthening legislation to facilitate enforcement of good corporate governance principles.

In short the corporate governance landscape in Zambia has improved significantly over the period 2000 – 2018. Clearly, much has been done, but much more remains to be done.

There is need for continuous director training and development in all corporate entities at all levels in order to ensure *sustainable boardroom effectiveness*. There is need for more corporate governance exposure for ministers in government; members of parliament and permanent secretaries, as representatives of the shareholders.

The impact of enhanced corporate governance practices in Zambia has been clearly manifested in increased investor confidence and greater foreign direct investment which has resulted in accelerated economic development in Zambia over the last 15 odd years.

IoDZ Corporate Governance Training For Audit Committees
Held on 21st November, 2013 at Grand Palace Hotel, Lusaka

SUMMARY

This chapter has demonstrated the economic benefits that are derived from embracing good corporate governance principles both at macroeconomic and microeconomic levels of the economy. Good corporate governance acts as a beacon to attract investors from both local and international levels and assures them that their investments are secure and efficiently managed in a transparent and accountable process.

Zambia has been cited to be a good example of the country that is reaping the benefits of practicing good corporate governance as it has experienced phenomenal economic growth on the back of increased investor confidence; for example, during the period 2000 to 2015 Zambia recorded an increase in foreign direct investment from around US$400,000 in 2005 to approximately US$4 billion in 2015 across sectors.

PART B
THE PRACTICE OF
CORPORATE GOVERNANCE

CHAPTER 8

OVERVIEW OF CORPORATE GOVERNANCE

DEFINITION OF CORPORATE GOVERNANCE

Further to the broad definitions introduced in the background section of this book, in a concise sense corporate governance is;

"The system by which companies and organisations are Governed, Controlled and Managed"
Cadbury Report, 1992.

ELEMENTS OF CORPORATE GOVERNANCE

Corporate Governance regulates the exercise of:
Power, Authority, Direction and Control, within an organisation, in order to ensure that the organisation's purpose is achieved on a sustainable basis.

This encompasses the following dimensions;

1. Creation and on-going monitoring of an appropriate and dynamic system of checks and balances to ensure the balanced exercise of power within an organisation;

2. Implementation of a system to ensure compliance by the organisation with its legal and regulatory obligations;

3. Implementation of a process whereby risks to the sustainability of the organisation's business are identified and managed within acceptable parameters; and

4. Development of practices which make and keep the organisation accountable to its identified stakeholders and the broader society in which it operates.

5. Development of structures, processes and practices that the board uses to direct and manage the operations of the organisation.

6. Defining how authority is exercised, how decisions are taken, how stakeholders have their say and how decision makers are held to account.

7. It deals with who is responsible for specific roles and responsibilities.

PRINCIPLES OF GOOD CORPORATE GOVERNANCE

The following are some of the main principles:

Integrity

Ensuring straightforward dealing and completeness, based on honesty, selflessness and objectivity, and ensuring high standards of probity and propriety in the conduct of the organisation's affairs and complaint decision making.

Responsibility

The Board of Directors are given authority to act on behalf of the company. They should, therefore, accept full responsibility for the powers that it is given and the authority that it exercises. The Board of Directors are responsible for overseeing the management of the business, affairs of the company, appointing the chief executive and monitoring the performance of the company. In doing so, it is required to act in the best interests of the company.

Accountability

Ensuring that all members of the organisation, including the office holder, staff members and members of any governing body, are seen to be responsible and accountable for their decisions and actions, including the stewardship of funds (with due regard to the independence of the office holder).

Openness and Transparency

Ensuring openness and transparency in order that stakeholders can have confidence in the decision-making and management processes of the organisation.

Effectiveness

Ensuring that the business delivers quality outcomes efficiently and represents good value for money.

Independence

Ensuring and demonstrating the freedom of the office holder from interference in decision making.

The relationship between the shareholders, the board, the management, employees and other stakeholders is at the centre of many of the problems that can arise in corporate governance. Many of the guidelines in the codes of corporate governance conduct and codes of best practice are directed towards reducing the potential for conflict, between the various stakeholder groups.

AGENCY PROBLEM

The separation of ownership and control in the modern corporation results in potential conflicts between the shareholders and the managers. In particular, the objectives of board and management may differ from those of the firm's shareholders. In large organisations stock may widely be held that shareholders cannot even make known their objectives, much less control or influence the board and management. Thus, this separation of ownership creates a situation in which the board and management may act in its own best interests rather than those of the shareholders and stakeholders.

In this case the board and managements are agents of the shareholders, shareholders hope that the agents will act in their best interests, thus, they delegate decision-making authority to them. To see how management and shareholder interests might differ, imagine that the firm is considering a new investment. The new investment is expected to have a favourable impact on the share value, but it is also a relatively risky venture. The owners of the firms will wish to take the investment because the share value will rise, but management jobs may be lost if management does not profitably manage the investment because of its risky nature. If management does not make the investment then the shareholders may have lost a valuable opportunity. This is one example of an agency problem which is simply a potential conflict of interest between the principals (shareholders) and the agent (the board and management).

To ensure that the board and management act in the best interests of the shareholders, the firm must incur agency costs, which may take different forms such as:

1. Expenditure to monitor managerial actions

2. Expenditure to structure the organisation so that the possibility of undesirable managerial behaviour will be limited and

3. Opportunity costs associated with lost profit opportunities because the organisational structure does not permit managers to take actions on as timely basis as would be possible if managers were also owners.

Corporate governance will, therefore, seek to harmonise the interests of the shareholders, the board, management, employees, and other stakeholders, as well as the interests of the community in which it operates. Corporate governance will also encourage the organisation to engage in consultative dialogue with government aimed at improving the policies, the rules and the statutory regulations guiding the administration and the operations of the area in which it operates.

Goal Congruency

As discussed in the preceding paragraphs, agency theory sees management as individuals each with his/her own objectives. Within a department of the organisation there is departmental objectives. If achieving these various objectives leads also to the achievement of the objectives of the organisation as a whole, there is said to be goal congruency.

In order for goal congruency to happen, appropriate incentives must be given and agents must be monitored. Incentives to be given include stock options, bonuses, and perquisites such as company automobiles and expensive offices and these must be directly related to how management decisions come to the interests of the shareholders.

Monitoring is done by bonding the agent systematically reviewing management perquisites, auditing financial statements, and limiting management decisions. These monitoring activities necessarily involve costs, an inevitable result of the separation of ownership and control of a corporation. The less the ownership percentage of the managers, the less the likelihood that they will behave in a manner consistent with maximising shareholders' wealth and the greater the need for shareholders to monitor their activities.

The Leadership Role

Essentially, governance addresses the leadership role in the institutional framework of the organisation.

The Board of Directors are squarely at the centre of this leadership role in the organisation.

WHY CORPORATE GOVERNANCE?

The interest in the systematic way in which companies and other organisations are directed and controlled is relatively recent.

In the corporate world, it was stimulated in the first place by concerns about fraud and later by the failure to correct evident managerial incompetence.

Recently, there has been more concern to facilitate investments and capital flows.

The last 25 odd years have seen a proliferation of corporate scandals and corporate failures all over the world including Zambia.

EXAMPLES OF CORPORATE FAILURE

Here are some examples from the Zambian scenario as well as from the international corporate world.

1. BANK OF CREDIT AND COMMERCE INTERNATIONAL, BCCI

On July 5, 1991, an incident that has been described as the biggest bank fraud in history came to a head when regulators in seven countries raided and took control of branch offices of the Bank of Credit and Commerce International. The scandal had been developing for nearly two decades and encompassed an intricate web of financial institutions and shell companies that had escaped full regulation.

The subsequent collapse of BCCI globally naturally led to the collapse of its Zambian branch and resulted in many depositors losing their money.

BCCI activities and those of its officers included dubious lending, fraudulent record-keeping, rogue trading, flouting of bank ownership regulations and money laundering in addition to legitimate banking activities. The lesson learned from this is the need for powerful executives and backers of institutions to be controlled within a secure enterprise-wide corporate governance structure, if the interest of other stakeholders, such as deposit holders are to be safeguarded, secondly the need for independent and unified regulation and auditing of complex financial conglomerates.

2. MERIDIAN BIAO BANK

When Meridian BIAO Bank was being set up the goal was to make it the dream commercial bank network for the continent of Africa hence the slogan, "Out of Africa and for Africa." On the contrary this promising PanAfrican Bank turned out to be short lived. One by one, central bank authorities in Zambia, Kenya, Swaziland, Tanzania, Gabon, and Burundi announced the closure or took over the management of their local Meridian BIAO as liquidity crisis engulfed the group. It was a far cry from the high hopes of its early days.

The lack of liquidity dogged the group from its early days and the founder Mr. Andrew Sardanis admitted that the bank's problem had been always been a shortage of capital. The liquidity problem appeared to have been compounded by the 1991 merger, and well informed sources had indicated funds were taken from the more profitable banks in English-speaking Africa to shore up less profitable operations in francophone countries (Gale, 1995)

3. ZAMBIA AIRWAYS

Zambia Airways was the only national airline which existed for three and half-decades. The airline had a lot of breaches of good corporate governance which affected its viability. For example, several times pilots would strike and airline staff benefits were routinely abused.

Government ended up owing the Airline vast amounts of money in unsettled airline tickets for government officials. This resulted in serious liquidity crises for the airline.

Furthermore, political interference led to some strange decisions as to who would run the line especially when it came to the appointment of the managing director. These and many other factors impacted negatively the operations of the company.

4. ZAMBIA RAILWAYS

Zambia Railways is the national railway company. Soon after becoming President of the Republic of Zambia in 2011, the late Mr. Michael Sata appointed Professor Clive Chirwa as the Chief Executive Officer of Zambia Railways. The action by the president to appoint Clive Chirwa was a direct breach of sound corporate governance practices. Good corporate governance assigns the responsibility of appointing the chief executive officer to the board of directors so that the appointee is answerable and accountable to the board. In the case of Zambia Railways, Clive Chirwa often acted as if he was not accountable to the board and this did not settle well with the board of directors. As a result, serious squabbles arose between the board and the chief executive officer which threatened the smooth operations of the company.

Clearly sound corporate governance had collapsed in the boardroom of Zambia Railways. The result was the dissolution of the board of directors and disappointment of the chief executive officer.

5. ENRON

Enron was a Houston-based energy company founded by a brilliant entrepreneur, Kenneth Lay. The company was created in 1985 by a merger of two American gas pipeline companies. In the year 2001, Enron became one of the 10 largest companies in the USA. Within the same year more and more evidence emerged about the weaknesses and fraudulent activity of corporate governance.

The role of a company's board of directors is to oversee corporate management in order to protect the interests of shareholders. However, in 1999, Enron's board waived conflict of interest rules to allow chief financial officer, Andrew Fastow, to create private partnerships to do business with the firm. These partnerships appear to have concealed debts and liabilities that would have a significant impact on Enron's reported profits. Subsequently, Enron's collapse raises the issue of how to reinforce the directors' capability and will to challenge questionable dealings through corporate managers.

Overall, corporate governance in Enron was weak in almost all aspects.

The board of directors of Enron appeared to have included a number of people who lacked moral character. They also appeared to be willing to engage themselves in fraudulent activity. This appears to have been the real cause of Enron's corporate governance failure and subsequent collapse of the company.

Most of these corporate failures have been traced to either the collapse or the non-existence of good corporate governance practices in the affected organisations.

Consequently, the focus on corporate governance achieved in the last 30 odd years has put corporate governance on the agenda of boards of directors around the globe.

Corporate governance has become universal because of its importance to building investor confidence, as well as transparent and efficient organisations across the world.

Ideals of Corporate Governance
Good corporate governance, therefore, seeks to achieve the following ideals:
1. Attract investors and donors – both local and foreign – and assure them that their investments will be secure and efficiently managed, and in a transparent and accountable process;
2. Create competitive and efficient companies, business enterprises and organisations;
3. Enhance the accountability and performance of those entrusted to manage organisations;
4. Guard against fraud and corruption.

Corporate Governance Challenge
It is against this background, that the need for good Corporate Governance for private companies, public institutions, banks and State Owned Enterprises, has become absolutely essential in all organisations round the globe, big and small.

The Five Pillars Of The Corporate Governance Equation
Corporate Governance is anchored on five essential pillars, namely:

1. The Shareholders
2. The Board of Directors
3. The Management
4. The Statutory Framework - *Companies Act and other attendant statutory instruments*
5. Other Stakeholders.

Stakeholders are all those individuals or corporate entities who could affect or be affected by an organisation's activities.
(*Cook & Deacon1999*).

It is vitally important that organisations identify their stakeholders and develop appropriate strategies to interact with each one of them.

SOUND CORPORATE GOVERNANCE PRACTICES

Good corporate governance requires sound corporate governance structures and processes to be put in place.

It also requires the installation of checks and balances to ensure that power is not abused.

This has implications for the composition of the board, the role and responsibilities of the chairperson, the role of the board, and the management.

Sound corporate governance also requires the board to be fully aware about *financial stewardship* and *accountability, strategic leadership,* as well as the *governance of risk* amongst other corporate governance issues.

DEVELOPING A SOUND CORPORATE GOVERNANCE SYSTEM

Ultimately, the board has a responsibility to formulate and install sound corporate governance systems to guide corporate governance practices in the organisation on a sustainable basis.

The following are the key corporate governance instruments that must be in place in every organisation:
   i)   A Board Charter
   ii) A Code of Ethics
   iii) A Strategic Plan, projecting 3 to 5 years ahead.

SUMMARY

An in-depth overview of corporate governance has been reflected in this chapter. Principles that constitute good corporate governance have thoroughly been discussed such as integrity, openness and transparency, accountability, responsibility, effectiveness and independence.

Examples of corporate failure which resulted from the breaches of good corporate governance principles from the Zambian scenario as well as from the international corporate world have been discussed. Some examples cited included Bank of Credit and Commerce International, Meridian BIAO Bank, Zambia Airways and Enron.

CHAPTER 9

THE ROLE OF THE BOARD, DIRECTORS AND THE LINKAGE WITH THE CEO AND MANAGEMENT

THE BOARD OF DIRECTORS

The Board of Directors, is a group of decision makers appointed by the shareholders (the owners of the organisation) who are given the authority to govern the organisation. The Board is the highest governing authority in the organisation.

"The Board's role is to provide Entrepreneurial leadership of the company within a framework of prudent and effective controls."
(United Kingdom Combined Code 2006)

In pursuing its key purpose, the board faces a unique set of responsibilities and challenges. The Board must:

1. Seek to ensure the company's prosperity (the directors duty to the company).

2. Collectively direct the company's affairs (entrepreneurial leadership of the company)

3. Monitor and control executive management (develop a framework of prudent and effective controls)

4. Meet its shareholders' appropriate interest (satisfy the agency element)

5. Meet its relevant stakeholders' appropriate interests (CSR)

6. Ensure the Board's moral and ethical commitment in areas such as bribery, corruption, political activity and gifts.

A basic requirement in corporate governance is that every organisation, be it public or private organisation, must have an effective board dedicated to ensuring that the organisation achieves its objectives, on a sustainable basis.

The board is the focal point of the corporate governance system.

TYPES OF BOARDS

Broadly speaking, boards can be classified into four (4) categories as follows:

1. PASSIVE BOARD:

These are boards that exist on paper only and hardly ever hold meetings. Decisions are taken by informal consultation by board members. These are common in privately held companies.

2. RUBBER STAMP BOARD:

These are boards that for various reasons lack the courage to challenge the proposed reasons from either head office or from shareholders. Rubber stamp board used to be common in State Owned Enterprises.

3. GOOD OLD BOYS BOARD:

These are boards whose members would normally be close friends or family members or rarely have appetite to discuss issues seriously and will always vote together.

4. EFFECTIVE BOARD:

As the name suggests this is the ideal board of directors.

Ideally, all Boards should aspire to be in category four!

The Effective Board;
- Has a balanced composition of professional skills, gender and age distribution;
- It is fully conversant with its roles and responsibilities;
- Discharges its responsibilities and acountabilities;

- Provides strategic direction and formulates sound policies;
- Develops the business;
- Delivers on its mandate;
- Has an effective and efficient company secretary able to help keep the board stay on top of its responsibilities.

SPECIFIC DUTIES AND RESPONSIBILITIES OF THE BOARD

The following are the main obligations and responsibilities of the board:

1. To appoint the CEO;
2. To appoint the Board/ Company Secretary;
3. To provide strategic direction;
4. To provide financial stewardship and oversight;
5. To monitor and evaluate corporate performance and the implementation of strategies;
6. To approve all acquisition and disposal of assets;
7. To provide oversight and monitor the management of key risk areas;
8. To ensure that there are adequate human, financial and other resources available to achieve the organisation's objectives;
9. To ensure that procedures and practices are in place to protect the organisation's assets, reputation and integrity.
10. To ensure that the organisation complies with all relevant laws and regulations affecting the organisation;
11. To ensure that the company has developed a succession plan for its executive directors and senior management.

DUTIES AND OBLIGATIONS OF INDIVIDUAL DIRECTORS

Directors are discouraged from appointing multiple alternate directors, as they are committed personally to Board responsibilities and obligations. Multiple alternate directors tend to be disruptive to the effective functioning of the board.

Each director should exercise all efforts to attend all board meetings. The duty of care requires that a director discharges his or her duties and responsibilities effectively.

A board member who has a real or prospective interest in any issue on the agenda, should declare such interest at a board meeting as soon as he or she becomes aware of such specific interest.

On first appointment and once every year, or at any time when circumstances change, all board members should in good faith, disclose to the board for recording, any business or other interests that is likely to create a potential conflict of interest.

LEGAL OBLIGATIONS AND LIABILITIES

Directors are in a position of trust (a fiduciary position) in relation to the organisation. Directors must act in a faithful, trustworthy manner towards, or on, the organisation's behalf.

In this fiduciary capacity, a director assumes two roles:
1. An agent acting on the organisation's behalf,
2. As a guardian or steward who controls the organisation's assets, on behalf of the shareholders.

It is vital that directors exercise their responsibilities carefully, as a director who is in breach of duty can be held personally liable for any loss suffered as a result.

Directors are personally and severally responsible for ensuring that the organisation complies with organisation's statutory laws.

They must also comply with a variety of other laws and regulations including employment law, health and safety regulations, the rules relating to payment of tax etc.

It is vital that directors exercise their responsibilities carefully, as a director who is in breach of duty can be held personally liable for any loss suffered as a result.

RELIEF FROM LIABILITY

Directors are protected by the presumption that they acted in good faith and in a manner they considered to be in the best interests of the organisation. This is known as the "business judgment rule."

They cannot be held liable if they voted against the decision that resulted in adverse circumstances;

Directors, however, remain liable for collective decisions, even after they have left the board.

ROLE OF THE BOARD CHAIRPERSON

The primary responsibility of the chairperson of the board is to ensure that the board is well run and performs its functions effectively.

The role of the chairperson is, therefore, critical to the success of the organisation.

In essence, this role relates to presiding over meetings and ensuring that meetings are well run and focused on the key issues.

WIDELY RECOGNISED DUTIES OF THE CHAIRPERSON

1. Providing overall leadership to the board.
2. Overseeing a formal succession plan or the board, C.E.O. and senior management.
3. Arranging for new directors appointed to the board to be properly inducted and oriented.
4. Maintaining sound relations with the organisation's shareholders and its important stakeholders.

5. Ensuring that all directors play a full and constructive role in the affairs of the organisation.

6. The chairperson should control the meeting, but should not dominate.

The Effective Chairperson should;

1. Understand the different personalities around the boardroom.

2. Have the ability to engage everyone at a board meeting and to know when to let the discussion ebb and flow.

3. Be a good listener.

4. Let the Chief Executive run the organisation and avoid attracting the limelight to himself/herself, whilst at the same time developing the kind of trusting relationship which allows him/her to act as mentor.

When all this is in place, a good chairperson never forgets that his/her primary duty is to the shareholders and to the organisation.

In summary, the chairperson should be a diplomat, a psychologist, a manager as well as a business minded person. Most importantly, the chairperson must be a person of integrity, who is able to lead the organisation as a sustainable business entity.

THE MANAGEMENT TEAM

The management team comprises, the CEO and all line managers and heads of departments, reporting to the CEO.

The increased global competition in the global business environment, consolidation, and innovation has created pressures that have influenced the emergency of management teams as basic building blocks of organisations. The economic, strategic, and technological imperatives are driving this transformation. There has been a shift from work organised around individual jobs to team-based work structures hence the term, *"Management Team."*

TYPES OF MANAGEMENT

Broadly speaking management can be classified into 3 categories as follows:

TOP MANAGEMENT

This is constituted by a small group of managers which usually includes a chief executive officer, or president with a few top senior directors. It is responsible for the performance of entire organisation through the middle managers. Unlike other managers, the top managers are accountable to none other than the owners of the resources used by the organisation. It should be mentioned here that the top management is dependent on the work of all, of its subordinates to accomplish the organisation's goals and mission.

MIDDLE MANAGEMENT

Middle management is second in ranking from the top, they are also known as the departmental managers such as *Director Operations* among others. Unlike first-line managers those in middle management plan, organise, lead, and control the activity of other managers yet, like first line managers, they are subject to the managerial efforts of a superior. In a nutshell, the middle managers coordinate the activity of sub units in the organisation.

FUNCTIONAL MANAGEMENT

The managers under the functional management are responsible for specific activities for example, production, marketing, accounting, and research and development.

SOME ROLES PERFORMED BY THE MANAGEMENT TEAM

1. Measurement of organisational performance in relation to set objectives.

2. Setting objectives for a given area of business activity in an organisation.

3. Perception of organisational problems and opportunities both from internal and external dimensions of performance.

4. Understand the consequences for an organisation, its present problem and opportunities through diagnosis.

5. Generation of action responses to the current problems and opportunities.

6. Analysis of the consequences for action recommended.

7. Choice of the preferred alternative course of action.

8. Programming and budgeting for the selected alternative course of action.

9. Directing and leading implementation groups, effective communication motivation and supervision.

THE DELEGATIVE AUTHORITY OF THE BOARD

1. The basic and fundamental role of the management team, headed by the CEO, is to carry out and implement the *decisions and resolutions of the board of directors.*

2. The board delegate's authority to the management, but doing so must not in any way result in the board and its directors abdicating their duties and responsibilities.

3. Whilst the directors are required to determine the future of the organisation and protect its assets, integrity and reputation, management are more concerned with implementing board decisions and policies.

4. Whilst the directors can be removed from office by the shareholders, senior management are appointed and dismissed by the directors.

5. Directors provide leadership and direction at the top of the organisation, whilst day to day leadership is in the hands of the CEO.

Differences between Directing and Managing

FACTOR	BOARD OF DIRECTORS	MANAGEMENT
MISSION	Govern and Direct	Manage and Control
ROLE	Trustee role	Agency role
KEY PERSON	Board Chairperson	CEO/MD
ACCOUNTABILITY	To shareholders	To the board
STRUCTURE	Ownership structure	Control structure
COMPOSITION	Majority of independent and non-executive directors	Executive management
RESPONSIBILITY	Strategic	Operational
GOAL	Shareholder value maximisation	Earnings maximisation
FOCUS	Strategy and sustainability	Enterprise risk management
CHECKS AND BALANCES	Audit committee External audit	Board committee Internal audit
REPORTING	Integrated reporting	Operational reporting
PLATFORM	Honesty with integrity	Honesty with integrity

Summary

Boards can be categorised into four broad categories as follows,

        1.   Passive Boards

        2.   Rubber Stamp Boards

        3.   Good Old Boys Boards

        4.   Effective Boards

The board has many duties and obligations which include some of the following;

- To appoint the CEO,
- To appoint board secretary,
- To provide strategic direction and
- To provide financial stewardship and oversight.

The different roles of the board chairperson, and management have also been thorough discussed in this chapter.

The different types of management and the general roles of the management have also been discussed.

CHAPTER 10

THE ROLE OF THE BOARD IN STATE OWNED ENTERPRISES

The term "SOEs" refers to enterprises or organisations where the state has significant control, through full, majority, or significant minority ownership.

At the time of writing this book the number of SOE's in Zambia had reduced from a peak of about 200 prior to privatisation to around 35 companies now, under the supervision of the IDC, as a *holding company*.

The State Owned Enterprise and its Purpose

In this chapter, I am going to address the following pertinent issues as regards the SOEs Boards;

The role of the board of an SOE vis-a-vis the enabling Ministry, board control of strategic decisions; even in instances where they may have an impact on economic policy, public policy and other national imperative, how government plays its role as a shareholder; whilst enabling the board to run the organisation effectively and how the board of an SOE achieves good financial performance whist simultaneously delivering on national priorities.

The chapter will also explain the obligation on SOEs to be more transparent and how SOEs can reconcile the need for public accountability and transparency with the imperative for commercial confidentiality.

It is critically important to keep in mind that it is in the Government's and the public's interest that all categories of SOEs are professionally run and adhere to good governance practices.

THE ROLE OF THE BOARD IN STATE OWNED ENTERPRISES

1. The boards of state-owned enterprises should have the necessary authority, competencies and objectivity to carry out their function of strategic guidance and monitoring of management.

2. They should act with integrity and be held accountable for their actions.

3. The boards of SOEs should be assigned a clear mandate and be accorded ultimate responsibility for the organisation's performance. The board should be fully accountable to the public and act in the best interests of the organisation.

4. SOE boards should carry out their functions of monitoring of management and providing strategic guidance, subject to the broad objectives set by government in general and the enablingMinistry in particular.

5. They should have the power to appoint and remove the CEO.

6. The boards of SOEs should be composed in such a way that they can exercise objective and independent judgment. Boards should also be composed of people with right skill sets.

7. Good practice calls for the chair to be separate from the CEO.

8. SOE boards should set up necessary specialised committees to support the full board in performing its functions, particularly in respect to *audit, risk management, remuneration and corporate governance.*

9. SOE boards should carry out an annual *performance self-evaluation* to appraise their performance as well as evaluating the standards of corporate governance in the organisation.

THE CHALLENGES FACING STATE OWNED ENTERPRISES

1. The governance challenge confronting SOEs has to do with creating a balance between governments' inclination to control public enterprises, and the commercial imperative to excel in their performance as business entities.

2. State owned enterprises face a number of peculiar complexities regarding their governance, which are not experienced in the private sector.

These include the following:

1. Board Composition And Appointment.

- Appointments to the boards of SOE's are made by the enabling ministry's minister in a non-transparent process unlike in the private sector where appointments are made through the nominating committee of the board.

2. Frequent Changes In Board Appointments.

- Very often changes at ministerial level are followed by changes in board appointments.
- Lack of complete autonomy and independence, in decision making.
- The invisible hand of government is ever present.

3. Reporting Relationships.

- The CEO of an SOE has multiple reporting relationships to the board, to the permanent secretary, to the minister and ultimately to parliament. This scenario can prove a nightmare to the CEO.

4. Political Involvement.

- Is never completely ruled out.

The need to satisfy a complex and often conflicting range of political, economic and social objectives.

The Unique Complexities of State Owned Enterprises

Against this background, the directors in SOEs will need to be mindful of the following:

i)   The *universal principles and practices of good corporate governance,* but should in addition be fully aware of the special complexities and sensitivities of SOE'S and the resultant multiple accountabilities.

ii) The fact that the success of an SOE depends on striking an appropriate balance between control and accountability on the one hand and performance and entrepreneurship on the other.

This is ultimately the objective of good governance, in a state owned enterprise.

Corporate Governance Workshop for State Owned Enterprises
3rd - 5th October 2011 - Hotel Intercontinental

SUMMARY

SOEs are enterprises or organisations where the state has significant control, through full, majority, or significant minority ownership.

Just like any other board, SOE board's role is to provide strategic guidance and monitor the management.

SOEs boards are confronted with two major challenges, the first one has to do with creating balance between government's inclination to control public enterprises and the commercial imperative to excel in their performance as a business entity.

The second challenge relates to the existence of multiple reporting relationships owing to the need to fulfil public policy requirements in the public sector.

CHAPTER 11

BOARD COMMITTEES

One of the fundamental responsibilities of every Board of Directors, is to establish *board committees*. The board chair should take a leading role in the establishment of appropriate committees of the board and in appointing the members of each committee as well as the chair of each committee.

THE ROLE OF BOARD COMMITTEES

    i)   Board committees are a mechanism to aid and assist the board and its directors, in giving detailed attention to specific areas of their duties and responsibilities.

    ii)   Board committees are better able to give a more comprehensive evaluation of specified issues, such as internal controls, audit, financial control, risk management, human resources and remuneration, and projects.

    iii)   Committees lighten the workload of the board thus allowing the board to handle more issues. This enables experts to focus on issues augmenting greater detail and efficiency when dealing with complex issues.

From a corporate governance perspective, a committee ensures that an issue gets adequate attention and that the board's independence and objectivity in making decisions is enhanced.

TYPES OF BOARD COMMITTEES

    1.   Some committees are standing committees appointed to perform a continuing function.

2. Other committees are short term with specific tasks such as investigating an investment opportunity or appraising a specific project. These are usually disbanded once the assigned task has been completed.

3. All organisations should have, at a minimum, the audit committee (Compulsory now under King III)

4. Industry specific issues will dictate the requirements for other committees.

5. The overriding principle is that boards must establish committees that are responsive to the nature of business and aligned as much as possible to the core strategic objectives.

Other committees that may be established, either as standalone, or in combination, could include the following:

1. Executive or Management Committee
2. Nominating Committee
3. Governance Committee
4. Risk Management Committee
5. Investment Committee
6. Finance Committee
7. Human Resource and Remuneration

It is the responsibility of the board to consider the committees appropriate for its organisation's purposes.

TERMS OF REFERENCE OF BOARD COMMITTEES

When establishing committees, the board must determine the following guidelines;

1. The terms of reference
   - the mandate and core objectives
   - specific duties and responsibilities
2. The composition of the members

3. Appointment of chairperson

4. Reporting procedures

   - Meetings, minutes and reports

5. The life span of each committee

It is imperative that the terms of reference provide:
1. Role clarity

2. Independence

3. Knowledge, skills and balance

4. Commitment

5. Appropriates

All committees derive their powers from what the board wishes to assign to them.

1. When establishing committees, the board should understand that even as it delegates some of its responsibilities to committees, the board remains the ultimate decision making authority retaining full responsibility for all board decisions,

2. The board should therefore consider all matters presented to it by the committees (taking care not to repeat committee deliberations) and apply both its collective skills and judgment to making decisions.

COMPOSITION OF BOARD COMMITTEES

Board committees should, as far as possible, only comprise members of the board. It may however, be necessary to co-opt specialists as permanent members of a committee, as where certain board committees fulfill a specialised role. This however, should be the exception rather than the rule and such specialists, should comprise a minority on the committee. A general safeguard should be that the quorum shall be formed only when at least 50% of those attending are members.

REVIEW OF BOARD COMMITTEES

The board should review all board committees annually, to determine the following:

- Whether any of the committees need to be restructured, modified, or scraped all together.
- Whether to establish new committees.
- It should be clear from the foregoing that no corporate entity can function effectively and efficiently without the existence of appropriate board committees.

SUMMARY

In order to allow for an effective and efficient board, it becomes necessary to create committees with various responsibilities. The types and compositions of these committees are set up according to the needs of the board; terms of reference defining and guiding committees are also set accordingly.

CHAPTER 12

CONDUCT OF BOARD MEETINGS AND ANNUAL GENERAL MEETINGS

DEFINITION OF BOARD MEETINGS

They are formal meetings of the board of directors of an organisation, held at a definite interval to consider policy issues and major problems. They are presided over by a chairperson of the organisation or his or her appointee, it must meet the quorum requirements and its deliberation must be recorded in the minutes. Under the doctrine of collective responsibility, all directors are bound by its resolutions.

The board of directors operates and makes decisions, normally through board meetings. In cases of matters that cannot wait until the next board meeting a round robin resolution can be approved and signed by directors except that such resolutions must be documented and presented to the next board meeting for ratification.

LEGAL POSITION

The board must follow the laid down legal requirements in making valid decisions, otherwise the board risks having their decisions overruled by the courts in the event of a subsequent legal challenge. The provisions of articles of associations guide the conduct of the board meetings. Therefore, it is imperative that every company has the articles of association in order for the meetings to be deemed legal.

REGULARITY OF BOARD MEETINGS

Good corporate governance [and King III] provides that the board should meet regularly for the purpose of conducting business.

1. A general rule is that a board meeting should be held once every quarter.

2. Extraordinary meetings can be called between normal scheduled meetings to consider special business.

PROCEDURE OF BOARD MEETINGS

For a directors' meeting to be held, it must be properly convened and properly constituted. The procedure is as follows:

NOTICE OF MEETING

A written notice must be issued by the company secretary at the request of the chairperson or another director but with the chairperson's approval.

1. The notice should give a reasonable period before the date of the meeting. 7-14 days is normally considered as reasonable.

2. The notice should clearly state the date, time, and venue of the meeting.

3. It is normal practice to schedule directors' meetings in advance for the calendar of the financial year.

4. The venue should be convenient to the directors.

AGENDA

1. The company secretary sets the agenda in close consultation with the chairperson and the CEO.

2. Directors wishing to have items included on the agenda should be accorded an opportunity to do so.

There should be a balance between the review of past performance and discussion of forward –looking issues;

1. Allow ample time for debate

2. Not too much time on routine or administrative matters.

The agenda and supporting board papers should be distributed timely in advance of the meeting, so that the directors can come prepared to make informed decisions;

1. Corporate world in general 1 – 2 weeks in advance
2. Minimum should be 1 week in advance

ORDER OF AGENDA

The following would be an example of an agenda for a Board Meeting:

1. Chairperson's welcome remarks
2. Quorum
3. Apologies
4. Appointments/Resignations
5. Declaration of Directors' Interests
6. Adoption of the Agenda
7. Minutes
   (a) Minutes of the previous Board Meeting (consideration and approval)
   (b) Matters Arising
8. Reports from the Board Committees
9. Management or CEO's report
10. Financial Report
11. Any specific issues (e.g. request for capital expenditure, new project).
12. Any other Business
13. Date of Next Meeting

REGISTER OF INTERESTS:

Members shall declare their interests if any in a register of interests provided for that purposes at every sitting of the board.

Duty to Disclose - A board member shall immediately report to the Chairperson of the Board any conflict of interest or potential conflict of interest and shall provide all relevant information, including information concerning his/her spouse and relative by blood or marriage.

The board member concerned shall not take part in the assessment by the board of whether a conflict of interest exists.

BOARD PAPERS

The board papers usually include the agenda, minutes of the previous meeting, a matters arising paper and reports as outlined in the agenda for discussion and particulars of any new resolutions for consideration.

Board papers should be;
- Short
- Timely
- Concise and Material
- Focused and action oriented

Board Committee reports should tender recommendations to the board.

DECISIONS OF THE BOARD

Decisions of the Board are referred to as resolutions.

1. An ordinary resolution may be passed by a simple majority vote of the directors present, whilst a special resolution requires the approval of 75% of the members present.
2. If the votes cast are equally divided, the chairperson will exercise a casting vote to determine the decision.

ATTENDANCE REGISTER

An attendance register must be maintained by the company secretary and must be signed by all directors attending the meeting.

PUNCTUALITY

It is considered best practice for directors to arrive at the meeting at least 15 minutes before scheduled starting time in order to network with other directors and to settle down.

THE QUORUM

A quorum is the minimum number of directors that must participate in a meeting for decisions to be valid.

Unless the Board Charter or other By-laws require a greater number, quorum for board meetings is usually fixed at 50% + 1 of the total board membership.

THE CHAIRPERSON

1. To ensure the independence of the board, the chairperson should not also be the CEO of the company.
2. The board chairperson will chair all board meetings. In his/her absence, the vice chairperson or another director, elected by the other directors will serve as chairperson for that meeting only.
3. While chairing board meetings, the chairperson should be mindful of possible conflicts of interest and deal with them in a transparent and effective manner.

The Chairperson's other responsibilities include:

1. Providing leadership to the board.
2. Maintaining liaison with key stakeholders including shareholders.
3. Introducing topics clearly.
4. Obtaining valid and pertinent contributions from board member.
5. Maintaining order.
6. Ensuring effective participation of all board members in discussions and decision making.

THE COMPANY SECRETARY

1. The company secretary is responsible for all administrative and organisational matters with respect to the preparation and conduct of board meetings.
2. The company secretary is responsible for notifying all directors of board meetings and for ensuring compliance with the procedure and the legality of Board meetings.
3. The company secretary is responsible for preparation and maintenance of minutes of all Board meetings.

4. Minutes of board meetings should at the very least contain

    i) Location and date of the meeting

    ii) Names of persons who participated in the meeting and those absent

    iii) Principal points arising during discussion

    iv) A record of board decisions (resolutions).

5. The Board Secretary also serves as the Chief Compliance Officer on Corporate Governance issues.

TIME FRAME FOR BOARD MEETINGS

1. Regular board meetings should normally last between Two-Four hours.

2. A *clear agenda*, timely submission of the *"Board Pack,"* and *"Committed"* reading of the board papers by the directors are key essentials for a smooth, timely and issue based board meeting.

DIRECTORS' REMUNERATION

1. Board members are entitled to be paid befitting directors fees for attending board meetings as well as board committee meetings.

2. Directors' fees are usually determined by the shareholders at an AGM.

3. Where a director attends meetings as a representative of another organisation, it is usual for the fees to be paid to the organisation they represent.

THE ANNUAL GENERAL MEETING

An annual meeting of the shareholders and directors of the company. A mandatory requirement of the Companies Act. Must be held once each year, within 3 months after the financial year end. Usually chaired by the Chairperson of the Board of Directors, even if he or she is not a shareholder, unless provided for otherwise in the Articles of the Company

Purpose of The AGM

1. To comply with the legal requirements of the Companies Act and the principles of good Corporate Governance.
2. To report to the shareholders on how the company has performed during the year.
3. Presentation of the annual report by the directors.
4. Presentation and approval of the company's audited accounts.
5. Election of directors in place of those retiring.
6. Appointment of Auditors.
7. Approval of proposed dividend on the recommendations of the Board of Directors.

Role of the Company Secretary in Relation to The AGM

1. The Company Secretary serves as Secretary of the Annual General Meeting.
2. The Company Secretary consequently prepares the Agenda and all the documents pertaining to the AGM and circulates to all the Shareholders.
3. The Company Secretary prepares minutes of all AGMs and maintains a minute book for this purpose.
4. The Company Secretary maintains a register of all shareholder's particulars and contact details.

Summary

A board meeting is a legally constituted meeting of the Board of Directors of an organisation. The Board of Directors meets periodically primarily to discuss and evaluate the performance of the organisation and to take decisions. These meetings are primarily for defined expectations of operational performance and holding management accountable to operational performance expectations.

The annual general meeting is a meeting of the membership or shareholders of an organisation. The annual general meeting is held to evaluate the performance of the board of directors, and to make fundamental decisions on the governance of the business. It is at this meeting where specific information required to be presented to the shareholders is tabled.

CHAPTER 13

THE GOVERNANCE OF RISK

Risk is the potential or likelihood that some threat, or threats, might occur to undermine your business or exploit any weakness in the business structure to cause loss or damage to the business agenda. Risk may be caused by either internal or external factors.

In the Zambian economic environment as in many other economies around the world, particularly in emerging markets, business risks abound which have over the years, led to the collapse of many corporate entities, in various sectors.

In the Zambian scenario, we have witnessed corporate failures in the banking and financial services sector. The earliest casualty in the financial services sector was Credit Organisation of Zambia soon after Independence. Others include Bank of Credit and Commerce International BCCI; Meridian BIAO Bank; Prudence Bank and Commerce Bank to name a few. In the non-banking sector, the list is even longer both in the private sector as well as in the parastatal sector. The largest category of casualties in the private sector has been SME's including family held companies.

RISK MANAGEMENT

What is Risk Management?

Risk Management is defined as, "The process of understanding and managing risks that an entity is inevitably subject to in attempting to achieve its corporate objectives."
(CIMA Official terminology 2005)

Risk Management Refers to:

1. The systematic process of identifying the risks that an organisation faces.
2. Understanding the nature of risks.
3. Evaluating the risks according to their likelihood of occurrence and the damage that could occur.
4. Deciding an appropriate action
5. Monitoring the risks.

It Also Involves:

1. Allocating responsibility for dealing with the identified risks.
2. Ensuring that risk management processes actually work, and;
3. Reporting material problems as quickly as possible to the right level in the organisation.

NATURE OF RISKS

There are several types of risks. These include the following:

1. New Risks

   Associated with new business activities.

2. Ever Present or Residual Risks

   Always around and constitute the majority of risks.

3. Contagious Risks

   A small risk may trigger other risks with catastrophic or damaging capability.

4. Sudden Risks

   These appear without warning e.g. accidents; fires; licensing changes; political shifts etc.

The cardinal rule in risk management is that you must know and anticipate your risks and be aware how risks may change over time.

CATEGORIES OF RISK

1. Strategic Risks

   These are risks of a long term nature with long term impact on the organisation. These include;

   - Reputational risks; changes in stakeholder relationships; changed assumptions; changes in political policies and legal systems.

2. Financial Risks

   These relate to risks with financial implications such as;

   - Liquidity; credit worthiness changes in interest rate; exchange rate; receipting, false accounting, inventory losses.

3. Operational Risks

   - Human resource; systems and equipment; legal and compliance; environmental and social events.

4. Natural Catastrophes/Act of God

   - Floods, fires, weather, earthquakes.

5. Fraud Risks

   - It focuses on risks associated with errors or events in transactions processing and other business operations.
   - Error of commission and omission sometimes done purposely.
   - Procurement processing is a major source of fraud.

METHODS OF MANAGING RISK

There are four broad categories of risk management, open to an organisation:

1. Avoid the Risk;

   This is the tranquil way for enterprises to manage their identified risks. In its simplest form, avoidance occurs when an enterprise refuses to engage in activities perceived to carry risk of any kind.

2. Transfer the Risk;

    In some instances, businesses elect to transfer risk away from the institution. Risk transfer typically involves taking out insurance against all major identified risks in the organisation by paying a premium to an insurance company in exchange for protection against substantial financial loss.

3. Reduce the Risk;

    Enterprises can manage risk through reduction which is meant to lessen any negative consequence or impact of specific, known risks, and is most often used when such risks are unavoidable.

4. Accept the Risk;

    Risk can also be managed through acceptance. Through this method, businesses retain a certain level of risk brought on by specific projects or expansion if the anticipated profit generated from the activity is far greater than its potential risk.

BUILDING RISK CONTROL MEASURES

When developing *risk control measures*, ensure that the measures are:
- i). Anticipatory in approach;
- ii) Preventive in practice;
- iii) Able to mitigate the effects of the risks if they should actually materialise.

Risk Management and Corporate Governance

"Risk management is an increasingly important process in business and it fits in well with the precepts of Good Corporate Governance."
(Cadbury Report 1992)

THE ROLE OF THE BOARD IN RISK MANAGEMENT

The overall responsibility for risk management lies with the Board of Directors.It is the responsibility of the Board of Directors to look after the assets of the organisation, protect the value of the shareholders' investments and the interests of other stakeholders. This includes a duty to take measures to prevent losses through error, omission, fraud and dishonesty.

Risk Management Committee of the Board

In order to adequately deal with risk management, the board should establish systems of internal controls and should review the effectiveness of the systems on a regular basis.

In order to undertake the functions of risk management, the board should appoint a group of their members to handle risk management.

This could be a *Risk Management Committee*, or the *Audit*, or the *Finance Committee* or a combination of either of them.

The Terms of Reference should be clear and detailed.
Functions should include;
1. Setting the board's risk appetite,
2. Monitoring implementation by management
3. Assessing the effectiveness of the internal audit department
4. Reporting to the board on internal controls and recommendations
5. Confirming that appropriate action is being taken

Where the role of risk management is combined, either with audit or finance functions in a board committee, there should be a clear distinction in the Terms of Reference relating to the Audit or Finance functions and that of Risk Management.

The board should know about and evaluate the;
1. Most significant risks facing the company
2. Possible effects on shareholders
3. Company's management of a crisis
4. Importance of stakeholder confidence in the organisation
5. Communications with the investment community

The board should ensure that:

1. Sufficient time is devoted to discuss risk strategy

2. Appropriate levels of awareness exist throughout the organisation

3. Risk-Management processes work effectively

4. A clear risk-management policy is published

5. Management should regularly report to the Board on the effectiveness and weaknesses of internal controls.

6. The Board should disclose in its Annual Report that it is accountable for the process of risk management and internal controls.

INTERNAL CONTROLS IN RISK MANAGEMENT

Internal controls are systems that are devised and enforced to ensure, as far as practicable, in given circumstances, the orderly and efficient conduct of business.

They include measures to;

1. Safeguard the assets of the organisation,

2. Prevent and detect fraud and error,

3. Ensure the accuracy and completeness of accounting records and ensure the timely preparation of reliable financial information.

SEGREGATION OF DUTIES

Wherever possible, duties should be split between two or more people, so that the work done by one person acts as a check on the work done by another. With segregation of duties, it is more difficult for fraud to take place, because several individuals would have to collude in the fraud.

PHYSICAL CONTROLS

Physical controls are measures to ensure the physical safety of assets, such as putting cash in a safe, securing cash receipts immediately and preventing unauthorised access to computer systems.

AUTHORISATION AND APPROVAL

All financial transactions should require the authorisation or approval of an appropriate responsible person. There should be an authorisation limit as to how much spending, each responsible person can approve.

REVIEWING THE EFFECTIVENESS OF INTERNAL CONTROL SYSTEMS

The review of risk management and internal control systems should be carried out at least once annually.

SUMMARY

1. Managing Risk is very different from managing strategy. It focuses on the negative – the threats and failures rather than the opportunities and successes.

2. It runs contrary to the "can do" culture that most leaders want to pursue when implementing strategy.

3. Many leaders have a tendency to avoid certain future problems that might occur down the road, hoping to pass them on to someone else's watch.

"In every single business failure of a large company in the last five decades, the board was the last to realise that things are going wrong."
(Peter Drucker – Managing for the future)

"It's only when the tide goes out that you learn who has been swimming naked."
(Warren Buffert – US Investor)

CHAPTER 14

BOARD PERFORMANCE EVALUATION

From my personal experience as a Corporate Governance Consultant, my observation is that many boards of directors in Zambia and elsewhere in the world for that matter, are not enthusiastic about subjecting themselves to a performance evaluation exercise and may even consider the process demeaning. Many "experienced" board members tend to feel that they are above being evaluated. Fortunately, this attitude is slowly beginning to change.

This chapter seeks to demystify as it were, the purpose, the objectives and the process of board performance evaluation in a way that brings out the positive intentions of the exercise as an important element of sound corporate governance practices.

The purpose of board performance evaluation is:
To ensure that the board performs to its maximum capability on a continuous and consistent basis and adheres to sound corporate governance principles and practices.

PEOPLE FACTORS AND PROCESS FACTORS
Board Performance Evaluation tends to break down into;
  i)   People factors and
  ii) Process factors.

People factors are, usually, by far the more important of the two in ensuring an effective board. In conducting a performance evaluation of the Board, consultants adopt a questioning approach to interrogate the corporate governance status of the organisation.

People Factors

Under people factors, typical questions would include the following:

1. How do the directors work as a team?
2. What are their interpersonal skills?
3. Is there a dominant or bullying chairman or CEO?
4. Is the chairman an effective leader?
5. Do all directors contribute?
6. What is the level of commitment, preparedness, engagement, absenteeism?
7. Is the board objective in acting on behalf of the organisation?
8. Is the board robust in taking and sticking to difficult decisions?
9. Are decisions reached by the whole board?
10. Do decisions take account of shareholders' views?
11. Are there 'unmanaged' conflicts of interest on the board?
12. Is the composition of the board being refreshed, is succession planning being practiced?

Process factors

In terms of process factors, the following are some of the specific issues and questions that should be considered in a performance evaluation of the board:

1. Has the board set itself clear performance objectives and how well has it performed?
2. What has been the whole board's contribution to the testing and development of strategy?
3. What has been the board's contribution to ensuring robust and effective risk management?
4. Is the composition of the board and its committees appropriate with the right mix of knowledge and skills sufficient to maximise performance in the light of future strategy?
5. How has the board responded to any problems or crises that have emerged and could or should they have been foreseen?
6. Are the matters reserved for the board the right ones?

7. What is the relationship between the board and the committees and between the committees themselves?

8. How well does the board communicate with the management team, employees and others?

9. Is the board as a whole up-to-date with the latest developments in the regulatory environment and the industry?

10. The processes that help underpin the board's effectiveness should also be evaluated e.g.

   i) Is appropriate, timely and unbiased information, the right length and quality, provided to the board and is management responsive to requests for clarification or amplification?

   ii) Are sufficient board and committee meetings of appropriate length held to enable proper consideration of issues?

EVALUATION OF THE BOARD CHAIRPERSON

The role of the chairperson is critical in any organisation and there are some specific issues relating to the chairperson which should be included as part of an evaluation of the board's performance. The following are the key issues:

1. Is the chairperson demonstrating effective leadership of the board?

2. Are relationships and communications with shareholders well managed?

3. Are relationships and communications within the board constructive?

4. Are the processes for setting the agenda working?

5. Do the processes enable board members to raise issues and concerns?

6. Are all directors encouraged to participate fully in board discussions?

7. Is the company secretary being used appropriately and to maximum value?

Performance Evaluation of Each Director

Performance evaluation of individual directors equally adopts a similar interrogative approach.

Accordingly, typical questions about each director would include the following:

1. How well prepared and informed are they for board meetings and is their meeting attendance satisfactory?

2. Do they demonstrate a willingness to devote time and effort to understand the organisation and its business and a readiness to participate in events outside the Boardroom?

3. How effectively have they probed to test information and assumptions?

4. Where necessary, how resolute are they in maintaining their own views and resisting pressure from others?

5. How effectively and proactively have they followed up their areas of concern?

6. How effective and successful are their relationships with fellow board members, the board secretary and senior management?

7. Does their performance and behaviour engender mutual trust and respect within the Board?

8. How actively and successfully do they refresh their knowledge and skills and are they up-to-date with the latest developments in areas such as corporate governance framework and the hospitality sector trends?

9. How well do they communicate with fellow board members and senior management?

10. Are they able to present their views convincingly yet diplomatically, and do they listen and take on board the views of others?

EVALUATION OF BOARD COMMITTEES

Generally speaking, with the exception of a few standard committees, such as the Audit Committee, Nominating Committee and the Finance Committee, all other committees should be subjected to regular review to establish their continued relevance to the organisation.

The evaluation of committees is similar and adopts the questioning approach described earlier. The following questions are typical:

1. Does each board committee have adequate, appropriate and updated written terms of reference?
2. Is the volume of business now handled by the committee (particularly the audit committee) set at the right level?
3. How effective are the board's committees, in terms of their role, their composition, and their interaction with the board?
4. Are board committees used to the best advantage?

KEY POINTS

Whichever methodology the organisation chooses to carry out evaluations, it is necessary to consider and clarify the following points:

1. Who has the overall responsibility for the process?
2. Who is going to have input into the process?
3. The structure and content of the process,
4. Most importantly, how the outcome will be acted upon by the board.
5. Overall, it cannot be stressed enough that it is essential that the purpose of board evaluations is to help the board perform to its maximum capability.
6. Finally, of course, it needs to be recognised that this is a continuing process, which must be conducted annually.

SUMMARY

In summary, the following points should be borne in mind in designing an effective evaluation system.

1.   The board as a whole should be part of the monitoring and evaluation process.

2.   Regular monitoring of the board focuses attention on good Corporate Governance.

3.   Any shortcomings should be addressed by either providing appropriate training *or* replacing the directors who may be found wanting.

4.   It is the responsibility of the chairperson of the board to conduct and drive the formal evaluations usually with the assistance of an external consult.

5.   Because of possible personal sensitivities, the chairperson should ensure confidentiality in managing the performance evaluation process.

CHAPTER 15

THE BOARD CHARTER

DEFINITION

A board charter is a policy document that clearly defines the respective roles, responsibilities and authorities of the board of directors (both individually and collectively) and management in setting the direction, the management and the control of the organisation.

Board charters have since become a standard tool of most boards and are recommended by most governance authorities including the King report of South Africa as well as the UK Code of Corporate Governance. Importantly, a board charter leaves a legacy from today's board to future boards and represents an important record of board policy making; but charters will only be value-creating if they are carefully crafted and used.

As a cornerstone of an organisation's governance system, the board charter needs to be treated as a living document, closely aligned with the strategic direction. It needs to be reviewed and updated regularly, and used as an important induction tool for new directors.

An annual review of any organisation's governance policies, including the board charter is recommended. Experience has shown that board charters are not among the most interesting documents of board membership and are easily overlooked, so the practice of annual review can be particularly useful. An annual review keeps the charter current and raises the directors' awareness of the organisation's overall policy framework. As such, the annual review of the board charter should be included into the board's calendar of activities.

Developing A Board Charter

In developing a board charter as a key governance policy, it is important that the board has the opportunity to discuss, elaborate and formulate the charter as part of the development process.

Broadly speaking, there are five stages involved in developing a board charter with a sixth stage for the board to undertake annually, as follows:

1. Meetings with key governance personnel, e.g. the chair, CEO and company secretary, to plan the process;

2. Document existing board policies and practices, and analyse the documentation collected;

3. Prepare materials for discussion;

4. Facilitate a workshop with the board to discuss the draft charter

5. Document the board's decisions in the board charter for final approval; and

6. The board or a committee of the board to review the charter annually.

Board Charter Development Process

In summary, therefore, the process should include the following elements:

1. Project Planning
2. Documentation Review
3. Prepare Draft Board Charter
4. Board Workshop or Discussion with Chair
5. Finalise Board Charter
6. Review after 12 months.

Key Components

Whilst the development and documentation of a board charter is generally unique to each organisation and reflects the specific nuances of the business, there are a number of core components that should be included in every such document. These include:

THE ORGANISATION'S VISION, MISSION AND VALUES:
A statement that defines the business and the principles that underpin all activities of the organisation. An essential starting point for creating the right culture in the organisation (however, success will depend on actions not words).

CODE OF CONDUCT:
Articulating behavioural expectations, decision-making process, compliance management and focus of the board;

THE STRUCTURE OF THE BOARD:
Clearly articulating what the governance responsibilities of the collective board are, structure and composition, sub committees and any external/ stakeholder relationships and lines of communication;

DUTIES AND RESPONSIBILITIES OF BOARD MEMBERS:
Details the specific and general expectations of individual board members; defining fiduciary responsibilities and individual roles and responsibilities;

COMPOSITION OF THE BOARD:
Defining the ideal board for the organisation - skill set, diversity (age, gender, culture) and knowledge and experience (always mindful of the laws of the land), tenure and succession plans;

PERFORMANCE MANAGEMENT:
Approach to individual and collective board evaluation and professional development, performance management of the chief executive and management of both these processes;

RISK MANAGEMENT:
The proposed structure to oversee risk, documentation of risk appetite and process employed to manage both the strategic and operational risks of the organisation;

MEETINGS:
Logistical details and expectations;

RELATIONSHIPS:
Between board members, the chief executive and
management and staff;

CONFLICT OF INTEREST:
How it is to be managed by both individual members and the organisation;
and

COMMUNICATION:
How a board manages internal and external communication will have a real
impact on the effectiveness of both its leadership and management; this
section provides the opportunity for the board and senior management to
think about this and create the communication strategy that aligns with its
business model and culture.

BENEFITS OF A BOARD CHARTER

The benefits of incorporating a board charter into an organisation's
governance system are fairly self-evident. The following are the key functions
of the board charter:

1. Documenting the policies that the board has decided upon to meet
   its governance, leadership, social and compliance responsibilities;

2. Providing a useful induction tool for new directors and senior
   managers;

3. Providing a reference point for disputes;

4. Removing individual interpretation from the decision making
   process;

5. Providing a forum and framework to discuss "difficult" governance
   issues; and

6. Creating a framework to review individual and collective
   performance and to clarify roles and responsibilities of both the
   board and management.

For new boards, the creation of a board charter during the formative stage of the organisation and the board, is acknowledged to be a very worthwhile experience and process.

For an existing board, if one is not in place, the same benefits can accrue and it is a relatively easy process to start and complete. If a charter does exist, then the annual agenda should include a review of its content and relevance on an annual basis to ensure it reflects the current policies and expectations of the board.

And finally, the board charter is not a secret document; its communication to stakeholders will have a positive effect and set the benchmark for performance, all of which has to be good for the organisation.

SUMMARY

The board charter promotes the highest standards of corporate governance within the organisation and clarifies among other matters, the roles and responsibilities of the board. It serves not only as a reminder of the board's roles and responsibilities but also as a general statement of intent and expectation as to how the Board discharges its duties and responsibilities.

The document is endorsed by the board and is subject to review by the board from time to time to ensure the organisation remains up to-date with the best practices in corporate governance.

CHAPTER 16

STRATEGIC PLANNING

The term 'Strategy' is derived from the Greek word "strategos" – which roughly translates to "generalship." The concept of strategy evolved from the science of war. During times of war, nations and allies developed a "grand" strategy with well-coordinated supporting strategies and tactics.

These war plans were called *strategic plans*. In the modern business world, a *strategic plan* can be defined, in simple language, as a set of actions or maneuvers directed towards the achievement of a specific goal, or set of goals.

Definition

Strategy has many definitions, but generally involves setting goals, determining actions to achieve the goals, and mobilising resources to execute the actions. A strategy describes how the ends (goals) will be achieved by the means (resources). The Board of Directors of an organisation is generally tasked with determining strategy.

Strategic planning is an organisation's process of defining its strategy, or direction, and making decisions on allocating its resources to pursue this strategy. It may also extend to control mechanisms for guiding the implementation of the strategy. Strategic planning became prominent in corporations during the 1960s and remains an important aspect of strategic management. It is executed by strategic planners or strategists, who involve many parties and research sources in their analysis of the organisation and its relationship to the environment in which it competes.

PURPOSE

In a concise sense the purpose of strategic planning is to set overall goals for the organisation and to develop an action plan to achieve them. It involves your stepping back from your day to day operations and analysing where the organisation has come from; where you stand now and where you want to go and setting your priorities.

In summary, a strategic plan is a road map to guide and direct the operations of an organisation and plays a critical role in ensuring continuity and success in institutional functioning and development.

Strategy includes processes of formulation and implementation; strategic planning helps coordinate both.

OVERVIEW OF STRATEGIC PLANNING

Strategic planning is a process and thus has inputs, activities, outputs and outcomes. This process, like all processes, has constraints. It may be formal or informal and is typically interactive, with feedback loops throughout the process. Some elements of the process may be continuous and others may be executed as discrete projects with a definitive start and end during a period. Strategic planning provides inputs for strategic thinking, which guides the actual strategy formulation. The end result is the organisation's strategy, including a diagnosis of the environment and competitive situation, a guiding policy on what the organisation intends to accomplish, and key initiatives or action plans for achieving the guiding policy.

STEPS IN STRATEGIC PLANNING

In summary the steps are as follows:
1. Environmental Scan and Situation Analysis
2. External Environment Analysis
3. Development of Vision and Mission Statement
4. PESTEL Analysis
5. SWOT Analysis
6. Formulation of Strategic Objectives

INPUTS

Data is gathered from a variety of sources, such as interviews with key executives, review of publicly available documents on the competition or market, primary research (e.g., visiting or observing competitor places of business or comparing prices), industry studies, etc. This may be part of a competitive intelligence programme. Inputs are gathered to help support an understanding of the competitive environment and its opportunities and risks. Other inputs include an understanding of the values of key stakeholders, such as the board, shareholders, and senior management. These values may be captured in an organisation's vision and mission statements.

ACTIVITIES

The essence of formulating competitive strategy is relating a company to its environment.

Strategic planning activities include meetings and other communication among the organisation's directors and management to develop a common understanding regarding the competitive environment and what the organisation's response to that environment (its strategy) should be. A variety of strategic planning tools (described in the section below) may be completed as part of strategic planning activities.

The organisation's Board of Directors may have a series of questions they want answered in formulating the strategy and gathering inputs, such as:

1. What is the organisation's business or interest?
2. What is considered "value" to the customer or constituency?
3. Which products and services should be included or excluded from the portfolio of offerings?
4. What is the geographical scope of the organisation?
5. What differentiates the organisation from its competitors in the eyes of customers and other stakeholders?
6. Which skills and resources should be developed within the organisation?

OUTPUTS

The output of strategic planning includes documentation and communication describing the organisation's strategy and how it should be implemented, usually referred to as the strategic plan. The strategy may include a diagnosis of the competitive situation, a guiding policy for achieving the organisation's goals, and specific action plans to be implemented. A strategic plan normally covers a period of 3 to 5 years and is updated periodically.

The organisation may use a variety of methods of measuring and monitoring progress towards the objectives and measures established, such as a balanced scorecard, logical framework or strategy map. Companies may also plan their financial statements (i.e., balance sheets, income statements, and cash flows) for several years when developing their strategic plan, as part of the goal setting activity. The term operational budget or annual plan is often used to describe the expected financial performance of an organisation for the upcoming year.

STRATEGY FORMULATION CHECK LIST

In summary strategy is a comprehensive plan which answers six questions as follow:

1. Where have we come from?
2. Where do we stand now?
3. Where do we want to be?
4. How do we get there?
5. How do we know that we are heading there?

Strategic planning has become a critical tool in sound corporate governance. No company, large or small, public or private, can in today's economic and business environment, afford to operate without a professionally prepared *strategic plan.*

In the Zambian scenario, as in other parts of the world we now have a good number of seasoned consulting firms, who are offering strategic planning services. There is therefore no excuse for any company in Zambia to be 'groping in the dark' as it were, without the enlightened assistance of an up-to-date strategic plan in hand.

Summary

Strategic planning involves setting goals, determining actions to achieve the goals, and mobilising resources to execute the actions.

The purpose of strategic planning is to set overall goals for the organisation and to develop an action plan to achieve them.

The output of strategic planning includes documentation and communication describing the organisation's strategy and how it should be implemented, usually referred to as *the strategic plan*.

CHAPTER 17

ETHICS AND INTEGRITY IN CORPORATE GOVERNANCE

Every institution, whether public or private, multinational or small and medium enterprise (SMEs) desires that what happens in their organisation, meets high ethical standards. Business leaders do recognise the pluralism of values and diversity of values of staff that exist in an organisation. Social norms and cultural beliefs have a bearing on one's moral obligation. In addition, the current environment of the player, that too, informs the decision making process of an individual. We are products of our environment.

This chapter discusses ethics and integrity in corporate governance.

Definition
We often come across terms like moral compass, ethics, unethical behaviour, lack of integrity. What do they really mean?

Ethics is a branch of philosophy which encompasses a set of moral principles that govern a person's or a group's behaviour. A moral correctness of specified conduct on which society can judge someone. Another definition of ethics is "going beyond what is legal and doing what is right, even when no one is watching you."

Consequently, when we talk about unethical behaviour in business, we are talking about actions that do not conform to acceptable standards of business operations, or failing to do what is right in every situation.

What Is Business Ethics?

Generally speaking business ethics refer to values and standards that determine the interaction of a business and its stakeholders. It identifies and implements standards of conduct in and for business that will ensure that its stakeholders' interests are respected. Business ethics are about what is good in terms of values and standards that guide the business in its interactions with its stakeholders.

WHY DO GOOD PEOPLE DO BAD THINGS?

Most professionals belong to professional associations like the accountants' bodies (Association of Chartered Certified Accountants, Chatered Institute of Management Accountants), Lawyers (Law Association of Zambia), Engineers (Engineering Institution of Zambia), Doctors (Medical Association of Zambia). Corporate Governance practitioners (Chartered Governance Institute, Institute of Directors). These associations have codes of ethics that govern the conducts of members in discharging their duties. Although companies and employees devote their time and energies to live up to these standards, difficult situations during the conduct of their business arise where they are called upon to demonstrate good behaviour. The tough choices that they have to make are called moral dilemmas. One of the most challenging issues for organisations today is unethical business behaviour. This behaviour has the potential to lead to a downfall of both an organisation and its leaders and therefore, it is important that it is dealt with utmost seriousness.

The following list constitutes some of the reasons that cause good people to do bad things;

1. *Business is warfare.* In today's business environment in Zambia when business opportunities are limited and competition is tough, some people are ready to   engage in unethical practices in order to get business/contracts;

2. *False communications.* Manipulation of financial reports for the purpose of portraying an organisation that it is doing well;

3. Breach of confidentiality;

4. Collusion, especially with competitors, to fix prices, is an unfair business practice today;

5. *Tax loopholes* are gaps in the tax codes that provide room for individuals or businesses to take wrongful advantage without technically violating the law;

6. *Pop Culture.* Highly qualified individuals, people who have had the best of university and college education such as lawyers, accountants, marketers, engineers, clergy, medical doctors, environmentalists etc. are now in the forefront in indulging in unethical business practices and the sad part is that they don't feel guilty about it and are sometimes crowned as champions. Competition and greed begin to drive 'success.' Society and business ecosystems join to glorify such as 'cool' and 'smart' and the age-old saying, *"Hard work is the key to success,"* has been replaced by *"Smart work" is the key to success!"*

7. *Pressure from Board or Management* by setting unrealistic and unachievable targets or pressure to meet business objectives;

8. Unquestioned Authority – the need to follow the boss's orders;

9. Peer pressure;

10. Personal greed and the desire for professional advancement;

11. Protecting one's livelihood;

12. One's personal moral compass i.e. values and standards;

13. Everybody does it. The false consensus, "Everybody does it," is a way for people to justify unethical behaviour. Stealing office supplies, and office time, falsifying documents and cheating on time cards are all unethical behaviours often justified by the person committing the act. Employing the phrase "Everyone does it," helps the wrongdoer not feel guilty about what he is doing, and it minimises the need to admit unethical practices;

14. Ignorance about company policies and improper training or ignorance that actions are unethical;

15. Working environment with cynicism or diminished morale;

16. The lack of consequences when caught such as sanctions.

The Table below shows examples of unethical conducts in different departments of an organisation.

Department	Likely Unethical practices
Human Resources	Hire unqualified staff, biased promotion and disciplinary actions
Marketing and Sales	False product advertising, lack of product liability, over promising
Finance and Account	Record falsifying/fraud, creative accounting
Procurement	Over invoicing, kick-backs, corruption
Quality assurance	Covering up product quality, fake products

How to prevent unethical Behaviour

Here is what you can do to help prevent unethical actions in your organisation:

1. Leaders in all organisations should face issues concerning unethical behaviour head on and should be ready to learn from each other about how best to tackle these situations;

2. It is important to build an "ethical culture and practice" in the organisation, at the Board and Management level;

3. Put controls in place;

4. Build a culture of transparency, openness, and communication;

5. Leadership *must walk the talk*;

6. Create a hotline for reporting unethical behaviour;

7. Create policies and practices by having an employee code of conduct;

8. Promote professional codes of ethics e.g. for accountants, lawyers, medical doctors, procurement, marketers and others;

9. Hire the right people by being objective and using psychometric software that determine human behaviour;

10. Develop people's understanding of unethical behaviour.

Examples of Consequences of Unethical Behaviour
1. Jail term according to the law; (individual)
2. Dismissal; (individual)
3. Company shutdown (organsation)
4. Bad reputation and reduced share-value (organisation)

BUSINESS INTEGRITY

Every profession has ethical standards that they follow. Integrity is an essential component of what every professional is expected to follow as part of the professional ethical behaviour, and is a much thought after trait. Certainly no patient would seek services of medical doctor who lacks integrity. Nor would a CEO hire a finance manager known to cook figures.

Although integrity is easily understood and noticed in our everyday lives, sometimes it is difficult to understand what it is, apart from assigning to it some traits e.g. honesty, truthfulness, dependability, trust etc. Integrity requires a high level of moral principles. Just as employers seek to hire people of high integrity, employees would also like to see that senior managers demonstrate high degrees of integrity. People who show integrity attract others to them because they are trustworthy and can be depended upon. It is a business requirement that business leaders lead a lifestyle of honesty, integrity, and high levels of ethical standards. Any poor judgment on their part may result in personal harm and bad reputation for the organisation that they work for.

THE ROLE OF THE BOARD IN BUSINESS INTEGRITY
Following an increase in corporate misconduct, Boards are now including business integrity as part of corporate governance. In practice this entails that directors, management and staff are expected to conform to specified high levels of ethics and integrity. This is usually enshrined in a *Code of Ethics*, document.

BUSINESS INTEGRITY IN SMEs

In most cases, when discussing corporate governance, the focus is on large organisations at the expense of SMEs. The reality is that SMEs are also exposed to the same risks as large organisations. While SMEs may not have the resources to have a business integrity policy formulated and provide oversight, by the nature of their operations, they are as prone to business misconduct as their bigger counterparts. Therefore, the rules of ethics and integrity apply to them equally.

Reporting and Protection Against Reprisals

At the operational level, there are several measures that an organisation may put in place in order to improve its business integrity. Internally, an organisation should devise a system of reporting of any suspected corporate infringement; either through a hotline established for the purpose or through an Integrity Committee formed at places of work, to the Chief Executive Officer (CEO) or any person designated to carry out an investigation and be able to sanction an erring employee. The action or inaction to be taken once a report has been made, may determine future levels of employee engagement in corporate integrity. The organisation needs to ensure that it deals appropriately with the employees concerned, but it also needs to consider what responses will increase the trustworthiness of the organisation. In other words, whether its response increases the likelihood that questions will continue to be raised; increases the likelihood that employees will come forward with concerns; and ultimately increases the likelihood that employees will know what the right thing to do is and will do it consistently.

PROTECTION OF WHISTLE BLOWERS

Any member of staff or stakeholder should be able to provide information to management if they see that someone has or is likely to commit a corporate offence. Once such a person reports, he should be protected against any retribution.

In Zambia the Public Interest Disclosure (Protection of Whistle Blowers) Act number 4 of 2010 is the applicable law. The Act affects both the public and private sector. It provides for both protection and remedies for a whistle blower. Section 10 provides for the protection of an employee who makes "protected disclosure or public interest disclosure". If a person makes an anonymous disclosure, that person must identify himself/herself to the investigating authority and that the investigating authority shall keep the identity of that person confidential. However, any such disclosure should not be frivolous or vexatious and is an offence and can be charged for criminal offence and liable to imprisonment for a period not exceeding seven years, with a possibility of a fine. The Act protects disclosure if it is made in good faith by an employee, the circumstance are reasonable to make such a disclosure and satisfies the following conditions;

1. That at the time of making a disclosure the employee who makes the disclosure has reason to believe that the employee shall be subjected to an occupational detriment if the employee makes a disclosure to the employer in accordance with section thirty-eight;

2. That, in a case where no person or body is prescribed for the purposes of section thirty-nine in relation to the relevant impropriety, the employee making the disclosure has reason to believe that it is likely that evidence relating to the impropriety shall be concealed or destroyed if the employee makes the disclosure to the employer;

3. That the employee making the disclosure has previously made a disclosure of substantially the same information to;

   i). the employer; or

   ii) a person or body referred to in section thirty-nine(39),

   in respect of which no action was taken within a reasonable period after the disclosure; or

4. That the impropriety is of an exceptionally serious nature.

Ethical issues or integrity in business is cardinal to both the individual working for an organisation as well as for the organisation as a whole. An organisation is made up of individuals who drive the processes and make decisions as to how they plan to conduct themselves. It is important that at the individual level employees should conduct themselves in an exemplary manner, while at the corporate level an organisation puts in place measures that reduce occurrences of corporate misconduct.

SUMMARY

Ethics refer to values and standards that determine the interaction of a business and its stakeholders. It identifies and implements standards of conduct in and for business that will ensure that its stakeholders' interests are respected. Business ethics are about what is good in terms of values and standards that guide the business in its interactions with its stakeholders.

CHAPTER 18

DYSFUNCTIONAL BOARDS

A well-functioning Board of Directors is key to the effective performance of companies and organisations, and their capacity to win the respect and confidence of stakeholders.

A dysfunctional board of directors on the other hand has the ability to cause multiple headaches for a company or organisation. Not only will a dysfunctional Board of Directors often fail to make decisions that are in the best interests of the organisation, its dysfunctionality has the potential to move outside the confines of the boardroom, causing negative publicity.

SIGNS OF A DYSFUNCTIONAL BOARD

In this chapter, I intend to display and discuss 14 signs of a *dysfunctional board* that I have come to observe in my experience as a Board member or as Chairperson of a number of companies over the last 40 years. These include:

1. Lack of confidentiality

    Much of what the board of directors discusses should be kept within the organisation. When board members do not keep this information confidential, problems often ensue. Leaking information is a sign of dysfunctionality within a board.

2. Conflicting Agendas

    Board members need to be on the same page when it comes to the future of an organisation and its initiatives. If Board members have conflicting agendas related to the direction of the organisation, it will be hard for the board to make decisions.

In addition to being on the same page with one another, board members must also be on the same page with the chairperson of the board.

3. Lack of Order

   Meetings involving the board of directors should function in an orderly manner. If board members quickly jump from topic to topic, argue with one another or fail to discuss the most important matters at hand, the board is dysfunctional. Board meetings should have an effective leader and a systematic agenda to make the meeting productive.

4. Lack of Respect

   Occasionally board members experience a lack of respect for the CEO of a company and vice versa. This often happens when board members have been in place for a long time and a new CEO enters the company or the other way round. All parties must develop respect for one another based on their common interest in working for the good of the organisation in order to keep the board from becoming dysfunctional. A lack of respect between new and older board members or factions within the Board can lead to a complete collapse of the corporate governance system in the organisation.

5. Hostile Environment

   A meeting of the board of directors can be a hostile environment, particularly when board members do not get along with one another. This type of environment stifles productivity and prevents Board members from sharing constructive opinions.

6. Secret Meetings

   While some information the board discusses should remain confidential, organisations should become concerned if a section of the board of directors regularly holds secret meetings or meet on an unofficial basis. Not only may some board members be left out of these meetings, but decisions could be made without the input of crucial members of the organisation, or with ethical motives.

7. Personal and Political Agendas

Board members should not allow personal and political agendas to cloud their decision-making. If board members continually propose moves that would benefit them personally or take a political stance, the image of the organisation could be compromised. Personal and political agendas also lead to avoidable disagreements among board members, and they are indicative of a dysfunctional board.

8. Lack of Trust

Employees in an organisation must trust the board of directors in order for it to be functional. If the majority of employees do not trust members of the Board, the advice and decisions of the board may be ignored or may lead to high staff turnover rates within the company, among other negative developments.

9. Dominating Members

Members of a board of directors should work as a team to make decisions to benefit the organisation, as a whole. The board's ability to make the best decision is compromised when one or two board members are allowed to dominate meetings. When certain members dominate meetings, you are looking at a dysfunctional situation.

10. Non-participants

Some board members sit on a board only for the prestige of being a board member. These members may attend meetings but rarely speak or offer any opinions for decisions. Too many non-participants around a board table spells "dysfunctional." The chair should ensure that there are no passengers on the board.

11. Power Struggles

Power struggles shift the board's focus from the business of the board to individuals or sub-groups gaining or maintaining "control." A board that is controlled by an individual or a sub-group is inherently dysfunctional. So, whether right or wrong about the issues, controlling the board is harmful; while use of vision, influence, knowledge and ideas is completely appropriate and desirable.

12. Board Micro-Management

Any board which seeks to micromanage the CEO and the management team will inevitably degenerate into a dysfunctional board.

13. Overly Powerful Executive

Sometimes executives amass so much "control" over the organisation that board members feel no need to do their job, or are reluctant or even too intimidated to openly question what is happening. Clearly, in these circumstances the board will have rendered itself dysfunctional.

14. Directors as "Representatives"

When directors act as representatives of their constituents rather than in the best interests of the organisation as a whole, difficulties will abound. Some directors go so far as to criticise the decisions of the Board to their constituents – a particularly disloyal and disruptive act.

All board members should, at all times place the organisation or the company first and to whom their total loyalty should be unquestionable.

The foregoing is by no means an exhaustive catalogue of what may constitute a dysfunctional board, but these have been some of the most common in my experience.

SUMMARY

A dysfunctional board of directors has the ability to cause multiple headaches for the organisation. A dysfunctional board of directors often fail to make decisions that are in the best interests of the organisation, its dysfunctionality has the potential to move outside the confines of the boardroom, causing negative publicity.

The signs of a dysfunctional board have well been discussed in this chapter.

CHAPTER 19

FINAL REFLECTIONS ON PRACTICE OF CORPORATE GOVERNANCE AND THE WAY FORWARD

From the foregoing analysis and discussion, it should be clear that the need for good governance is now internationally recognised. This is because of the high correlation between corporate governance and investor decisions. If the management of the economic and social resources for development in a country is efficient and there is transparency and accountability in the government, there is likely to be high levels of private sector investment inflows into the country. Good corporate governance improves the financial performance of companies and the capital markets. Efficient companies will inevitably lead to stronger economies.

As countries face the global market, national economic policy makers will need to understand and to be aware of the effect of poor corporate governance on companies. In many developing countries where a significant proportion of previously state owned companies have been privatised, and where increasing numbers of companies are being established, the private sector would seem to hold the key to the economic growth and development of these countries.

Governments in developing countries must create an enabling environment for the private sector to spearhead economic development while at the same time encouraging the participation of all stakeholders in development. There is need to extend and apply corporate governance principles to a wide range of organisations, and not just the publicly listed joint stock companies. Such organisations include the banking sector, state enterprises, co-operatives, and the growing and increasingly important NGO sector. Efficiency, transparency and accountability are essential to achieving sustainable development.

Whilst the preoccupation of the corporate governance debate has tended to focus on the issues relating to the conformance of boards of companies to high standards of transparency, probity, accountability and responsibility, I hold the view that issues relating to the performance of company boards to provide the necessary strategic leadership which will sustain their companies' competitiveness in the global market should be included in the debate. Equally important is the need for a consensus, which maintains the harmonious and productive relationships between the company and its host society.

In addition, professional institutions form an essential fabric of a modern economy, and good institutional infrastructure is now vital as good physical infrastructure. The solution must rest in the provision of appropriate training for directors.

Just as institutes of *accountancy, law, medicine and engineering* all work to set standards and accredit their own professionals, so too should Institutes of Directors and management colleges help train and ultimately accredit directors thereby changing directorship from a status to a profession.

A WORD ON CORRUPTION

Corruption is an enemy to good corporate governance and is an issue which all countries and, especially the developing economies must address if the benefits of good governance are to have any effect at all. Whilst corruption is not unique to the developing countries, nevertheless, it has crippling effects on these countries because these economies are small and vulnerable to global vagaries.

FROM NATIONALISATION TO CORPORATE GOVERNANCE

Let me now attempt to summarise the *corporate governance* genesis in Zambia over the last 20 odd years as a basis for charting the way forward. There is little doubt that significant strides have been made in Zambia towards advancing the frontiers of corporate governance in the country. Credit is due to the Institute of Directors of Zambia for the pioneering role that the organisation played in setting the pace for corporate governance reform in the country and in particular the positive changes that have taken place over the years in the governance of State Owned Enterprises.

In a period of less than 20 years, from the 1990s Zambia has discernibly moved from nationalisation to corporate governance.

As I observed in chapter 1, until the beginning of the 1990s, little was known about corporate governance in Zambia largely as a result of the structure of the Zambian economy prior to this period.

It will be recalled that following the Mulungushi Economic Reforms of 1968, Zambia nationalised nearly all industries and economic entities in general, including the mining companies in which the state acquired majority shareholding. Under the policy of nationalisation the government created economic superstructures, under ZIMCO, INDECO, etc. that directly controlled and supervised all State Owned Enterprises.

The liberation of the economy and the privatisation process that followed in the early 1990s, signaled the beginning of the development of corporate governance in Zambia.

The birth of the IoD Zambia in the landmark year 2000 has really served as the greatest catalyst in the development and growth of corporate governance in Zambia.

To its credit, IoD Zambia has been at the forefront of rolling out corporate governance reform over the last 20 odd years. IoD Zambia has managed to develop a respectable working relationship with successive governments which have facilitated the process of initiating the infusion of sound corporate governance practices in the public sector. In particular, the administration of Late Republican President, Levy Mwanawasa was most progressive in embracing corporate governance reforms.

Alongside, institutional reform, the IoD also rolled out an aggressive director training programme which has seen over 3,000 directors from both the public sector and the private sector being trained in various aspects of corporate governance as well as in understanding the role of a director, in corporate affairs.

THE GREATEST CHALLENGE

Whilst the pace of corporate governance exposure and practice in the private sector, can be described as progressing at good pace, it is fair to state that the most pronounced challenge, or to put it in another way, the most apparent failure of corporate governance reform remains manifest in the surviving State Owned Enterprises.

Successive Auditor General's reports continue to reflect disturbing lapses in the way public sector entities are being managed. As an example, 27 named institutions had not produced audited financial statements for the financial years up to 31st December, 2015 in contravention of their enabling Statutory Instruments, as well as the tenets of good corporate governance.

The Auditor General's report further exposed glaring irregularities and poor corporate governance practices. Some of the issues raised were poor financial and operational performance, relatively little awareness of Corporate Governance Systems, weak enforcement, transparency, and unsatisfactory succession planning.

BOARD APPOINTMENTS AND BOARD TENURE IN SOEs

I have stressed the point earlier in this book that, the board, is the focal point of the corporate governance system. The success or failure of an organisation largely depends on the effectiveness of its board of directors.

It is unfortunate therefore to observe that with regard to State Owned Enterprises, the issue of Board appointments and board tenure still remains one of the weakest points.

Whilst we have observed a major positive structural change in the manner Chairperson's of Boards of Directors of SOE's are appointed, regrettably, the manner in which board tenure is handled still leaves a lot to be desired, in terms of Corporate Governance principles.

During the First and Second Republic under President Kenneth Kaunda, all chairpersons of SOE boards of directors, were appointed from either cabinet ministers or permanent secretaries. The reality is that these appointments continued under President Fredrick Chiluba. Real Corporate Governance reform in the Public sector was introduced under the Administration of President Levy Patrick Mwanawasa, the second President under the MMD regime. The old system was progressively done away with and today all SOE boards in Zambia are chaired by independent directors from the private sector. This is a very significant development in terms of promoting checks and balances and enhancing transparency, in State Owned Enterprises.

On the other hand, the appointment of board members in SOE's still remains subjective in the hands of sector cabinet ministers. This has tended to lead to board tenure instability which in turn disrupts sustainable application of sound Corporate Governance principles and practices.

It has become fairly common practice in Zambia today to expect the Boards of SOE's to be dissolved soon after a new sector cabinet minister is appointed. Usually no credible reasons are assigned and it does not matter whether a board is as young as a few months old.

A classical case worth citing is the double dissolution of ZICTA and ZAMPOST Boards through a press statement dated 25th November, 2019, and announced on ZNBC and other local media houses on the same day. This particular press statement read as follows:

"In accordance with (section 4) part 1 of the Zambia Information and Communications Authority (ZICTA) Act No. 15 of 2009, and powers vested in me thereof, I have decided to dissolve the Board of ZICTA with immediate effect.

146

Further, in accordance with the first schedule (section 3) of the Postal Services Act, I have decided to dissolve ZAMPOST Board with immediate effect.

I want to take this opportunity to thank the outgoing members of the ZICTA and ZAMPOST Boards, for their contribution to the nation while serving as members of the boards during their tenure.

I wish them well in their future endeavours."

Minister of Transport and Communication

Needless to say that this practice is retrogressive and needs to be addressed, for example, by borrowing a leaf from the Namibian policy decision in this similar area of concern.

Indeed, Zambia and many other African countries could benefit from adopting a new system that has recently been introduced in Namibia with regard to the appointment of board members of State Owned Enterprises. Up until recently the appointment of SOE board members in Namibia followed exactly the same system, currently obtaining in most African countries including Zambia, whereby cabinet ministers have complete autonomy on the appointment and firing of board members.

Namibia has made a ground breaking policy decision, which was announced by the country's Minister of Public Enterprises, Leon Jooste on 2nd September, 2019.

Drawing on the country's Public Enterprises Governance Act 2019, Namibia has introduced a new policy under which all board members of SOE's are now being effected through an open and transparent system. Under the new system, all board positions are now required to be advertised in the media and those short listed are then interviewed by a panel of specialists to select the best candidates.

147

Once board members have been selected through this process, board chair and vice chair are then elected by all the board members themselves for an initial period of three years.

The new system has had the effect of not only making it possible for the most suitable candidates to be appointed to the boards of SOE's, but it has also removed negative patronage and subjectivity associated with the old system. The loyalty of the board members now lies squarely with the organisations that they serve and not to appointing authorities. It is also likely to result into more stable and sustainable boards and thus strengthening the strategic performance of the SOE's in Namibia.

THE LUSAKA SECURITIES EXCHANGE

One of the positive corporate governance developments in the last 20 years has been the establishment of the Lusaka Securities Exchange (LuSE). Apart from contributing to the deepening Zambia's capital markets, the LuSE, although comparatively small with a current total market capitalisation of around US$ 5 billion, is a significant step towards strengthening corporate governance practices. To this end LuSE has published corporate governance compliance guidelines for all listed companies. Listed companies need to enhance their standards of corporate governance so that they can equate to international standards.

THE NEW COMPANIES ACT NO. 10 OF 2017

A new Companies Act No. 10 of 2017 has been enacted and has already come into force. Up until now corporate governance compliance has remained voluntary in Zambia. The approach to corporate governance compliance has simply been, "comply or explain" - period.

The enactment of this new law follows the pattern that has been implemented in other progressive assets.

South Africa, for instance took this step in 2008 when a new Finance Act was enacted to incorporate many provisions of the 4 King Reports on Corporate Governance.

148

Zambian's New Companies Act, 2017 essentially seeks to address the following:

1. To cure the shortcomings of the Old Companies Act Cap 388 by addressing inadequate provisions on corporate governance such as the limited safeguards against abuse of powers by directors and insufficient measures to foster transparency.

2. Elaborating the duties and responsibilities of company secretaries.

3. Outlining director's duties such as duty to act honestly, in good faith and in the best interest of the company and to exercise care, diligence and skill.

4. Generally weak legal and regulatory insolvency framework.

5. Foster transparency and high standards of Corporate Governance by prescribing functions and obligations of directors and Company Secretaries.

6. Align Company Law with other pieces of legislation, international based practice and bring it in tandem with technological developments.

7. Strengthen financial reporting and corporate governance.

8. Seal loopholes and prevent the abuse of corporate bodies for illegal activities.

9. Separating insolvency provisions and placing them in a separate statute the *Corporate Insolvency Act*, and thus enhancing the regulating framework for insolvency practitioners.

THE PUBLIC FINANCE MANAGEMENT ACT NO. 1 OF 2018

The Public Finance Management Act No. 1 of 2018 was enacted to provide for the following:

i). Institutional and regulatory framework for management of public funds;

ii). Strengthening of accountability, oversight, management and control of public funds in the public financial management frame work;

iii). Responsibilities and fiduciary duties of controlling officers and controlling bodies;

iv) Enhancement of cash management systems to ensure efficient and effective utilisation of cash for the Government;

v) The processes for efficient production of the Financial Report for the Republic and

vi) The management and control of public assets and stores.

Current IoDZ President, Mrs Victoria Silutongwe with Former IODZ President, Mr Mumba Kapumpa, SC. at a directors' event.

*Mr. Patrick. D. Chisanga with the first interim President of the IoDZ (2000 -
2001), Mr. Stephen Ndhlovu, at the launch of the IoDZ Strategic Plan, 2020 -
2023, on 19th December, 2019, at the Southern Sun Hotel, Lusaka.*

EPILOGUE

Let me conclude by restating what I said in my introductory remarks and that
is, I sincerely hope that this book will serve two purposes:

Firstly, I hope that it will provide a fairly authoritative account of the
development and growth of Corporate Governance in Zambia and may
consequently be of use to historians on the subject.

Secondly, I hope that the book will serve as a reliable reference for students
and practitioners of Corporate Governance, alike.

Looking back over the last 20 odd years, I think it is fair to state that much
has been done to advance the frontiers of Corporate Governance in Zambia.

However, I do hasten to add that a lot more remains to be done, including
strategic entrenchment of strong transformational mind-set and practices
through Transformational Leadership Development Programmes as
previewed in the following final chapter (20) dedicated to the amazing story
of Zambian Institute of Leadership.

CHAPTER 20

PREAMBLE

The need to raise *transforming leaders of integrity* who serve as trusted stewards of public and private responsibilities and resources; and humbly handle power, privileges and positions of leadership, is critical to Africa's transformation. Zambia can be positively transformed by *discovering, developing and deploying transforming leaders of integrity*. Improved leadership is evidently an essential part of Zambia's economic, political, moral and social development given the vast resources with which we have been endowed.

First world nations like the United States of America and Singapore understood and embraced the *need to commission learning and leadership institutes* that would develop transformational leaders to drive and deliver success and generational posterity to their succeeding epochs.

The past and current trends of educational and professional development in most African countries, Zambia inclusive, attest to the fact that transforming leadership development is more often an after-thought activity which is not always prioritised in the allocation of resources at national and organisational levels. It is this trend that has led to *perpetual lack of critical mass of transforming leaders of integrity* with the competencies and capacity to lead holistic national transformation in African countries.

BACKGROUND OF ZAMBIAN INSTITUTE OF LEADERSHIP (ZIL)

In my diverse and long years of practicing and consulting on Corporate Governance in Zambia and beyond, one major common and recurrent comment

I have received from Corporate and non-corporate Executives is the request for leadership training to help them lead their organisations most effectively. Snr. Chief Mumena of the North Western Province of Zambia is among the key leaders from Zambia who have persistently urged me to do something about leadership development programme in Zambia.

It is within the above context that I began dreaming and putting together a team of professionals with the similar quest to contribute to Zambia's and Africa's transformational leadership agenda.

The driving ethos of this team of professional women and men (Founding ZIL Board of Directors) was to specifically focus on building leaders of integrity across the various disciplines; with the belief that effective leadership is key for the success of any institution and ultimately sustainable development.

The team's efforts brought forth the first ever Zambian Institute of Leadership (ZIL) which is wholly focused on creating leadership value at various levels in Zambia and Africa.

PROCESSES LEADING TO SUCCESSFUL ESTABLISHMENT OF ZIL

The journey towards the successful incorporation and operationalisation of ZIL was not easy and hence required huge sacrifice and investment of long hours by all team members. The following are the summary description of the key processes that we went through in establishing ZIL:

i)   Development of the Concept Paper on ZIL;
ii) Deliberations and adoption of the Concept Paper
iii) Constitution of ZIL Board of Directors,
iv) Development of ZIL Articles of Association
v)   Deliberations and adoption of ZIL Articles of Association
vi) Registration of ZIL with PACRA as a Private Company Limited by Guarantee

vii) Development of the ZIL Board Charter

viii) Deliberations and adoption of ZIL Board Charter

ix) Appointment of the Interim ZIL Executive Management Team

x) Opening of the ZIL Bank Account

xi) Constitution and operationalisation of ZIL Board Committees

xii) Development of the First Strategic Plan for ZIL

xiii) Piloting on selected leadership development programs in collaboration with some strategic partners.

OFFICIAL ZIL LAUNCH CEREMONY

The Minister for Higher Education, Mr. Brian Mushimba, representing Her Honour, the Vice President, Ms. Inonge Wina, officiated the launch of ZIL. In his introductory remarks, Mr. Mushimba took some time to appreciate and endorse the initiative of ZIL as a timely venture in respect to the need to develop leaders of integrity for Zambia. Of particular interest and emphasis was his personal story on how a similar leadership mentorship he had gone through in the past, was instrumental in catapulting him to the various regional and national roles and responsibilities both within and beyond the Zambian boundaries.

In her speech the Republican Vice President recognised that structured and long-term focused development of transformational world class leaders was the need of the hour. She appreciated the special place and role that ZIL will play in collaboration with Public and Private Sector leaders in order to make Zambia more progressive and harmonious.

The Vice President expressed her abiding faith in the future fortunes of the Republic of Zambia that are predicated on providing local solutions in order to meet the challenges of our times; the prerequisite to this change, she indicated, would be ignited by having transformational leaders of integrity in all spheres of economic strata. She emphasised that Zambia needs a new cadre of leadership that will inspire its people to become global leaders in the fields of science, technology, engineering, mathematics, innovation, music, art and sports; and that if Zambia is to leapfrog many development phases and begin to compete on the global platform, it needs to grow leaders with a global mindset and who think generational.

154

Both the Vice President of the Republic of Zambia and the Minister for Higher Education welcomed ZIL to consider further engagements that would make the Government of the Republic of Zambia benefit from the ZIL leadership programmes and services.

The ZIL launch was attended by distinguished Corporate leaders and professionals from the Public and Private Sectors, the Diplomatic Community, Civil Society Organisations, Religious Institutions and Media Houses, most of whom their names have been enclosed in the appendices section of this book.

LIST OF FOUNDING BOARD OF DIRECTORS FOR ZIL

	NAME OF ZIL BOARD MEMBER	DESIGNATION
1	Mr. Patrick D. Chisanga	Member/Chairperson
2	Ms. Engwase B. Mwale	Member/Vice Chairperson
3	Mr. Chibamba Kanyama	Member
4	Eng. Bernard Chiwala	Member
5	Mr. Dev Haman	Member
6	Dr. Ntombi Mudenda	Member
7	Dr. Ebby Mubanga	Member
8	Ms. Chitupa Mung'omba	Member
9	Mr. George Arudo	Member/Acting Executive Director
10	Mr. Norman Siwila	Board Secretary

VISION OF ZIL

Generations of world-class transformational leaders of integrity, positively impacting on the economic, political and social development of Zambia and other African nations.

MISSION STATEMENT OF ZIL

To ignite and accelerate the discovery and development of generations of transformational leaders of integrity through long term commitment and implementation of various capacity building initiatives.

GUIDING VALUES OF ZIL

- Culture of Integrity
- Transparency and Accountability
- Team Work
- Professionalism
- Gender Equity and Equality
- Commitment
- Excellence
- Inclusivity

STRATEGIC OJECTIVES OF ZIL UNDER THE 2020-2024 STRATEGIC PLAN

1. Programmes and Services Perspective

   - To design leadership development programmes and content, structured for each of the identified sectors by June, 2020.

   - To develop a pool of 30 Facilitators in Transformational Leadership, Professional Coaching and Youth Leadership by December, 2020.

   - To conduct at least 10 training programmes in Transformational Leadership, Professional Coaching and Youth Leadership from the pool of identified stakeholders per calendar year through the Strategy period.

   - To initiate and build formal collaborative partnerships with local and international organisations in the field of Leadership Development through the Strategy period.

2. Marketing and Growth Perspective

   - To develop, adopt, implement and monitor ZIL's Marketing Strategy for the institution's growth and development through the Strategy period.

3. Financial and Administration Perspective

   - To develop, adopt, implement and monitor ZIL's Resource Mobilisation Strategy for the Institution's growth and sustainability to deliver on its mandate through the strategy period

- To develop, adopt, implement and monitor key Finance and Administration policy documents for ZIL's institutional efficiency and effectiveness through the Strategy period.

- To develop and implement a comprehensive ICT system that would harness both internal and external capacity for ZIL's effective delivery of services through the Strategy period.

Partnership with ZIL Programmes in Enhancing Corporate Governance

Having established all the key structures and systems necessary for its historic take-off, ZIL has begun by collaborating with various professional bodies in offering diverse range of World-class Leadership development programs to the Corporate and non-corporate leaders and executives in Zambia and beyond. For example, Dynamic Concepts Ltd and International Leadership Foundation –(ILF) Zambia have co-embarked with ZIL on this legacy – driven initiative.

It is this collaborative approach with other like-minded entities and individuals that will accelerate the process of holistic (social, economic, political, moral etc.) and legacy – driven transformation at personal, organisational and national levels. The process of identifying, developing and deploying transformation- minded leaders in strategic societal domains of leadership is very integral and core mandate of ZIL.

ZIL Board of Directors and the Management Team are ready to avail themselves in supporting all the practitioners of Corporate Governance, by equipping them with world –class transformational leadership skills and experiences. We strongly believe that ZIL is poised to make a legacy of raising the bar in regard to enhancing high levels of integrity and ethics in the practice of leadership, Corporate Governance and organisational management in Zambia and beyond.

ZIL passionately looks forward to receiving you when you knock at our doors; being received by you when we knock your doors; and ultimately working with you in building world-class transformational leaders of integrity for your organisation!

Mr. Patrick D. Chisanga in the middle, front row on his left/right, the Minister for Higher Education, Mr. Brian Mushimba and other guests at the official launch of ZIL on 13th December, 2019 at Mulungushi International Conference Centre, Lusaka

LIST OF ACRONYMS

ACCA - Association of Chartered Certified Accountants
ACGN - African Corporate Governance Network
AGM - Annual General Meeting
BCCI - Bank of Credit and Commerce International
CACG - Commonwealth Association for Corporate Governance
CCO - Chief Compliance Officer
CEO - Chief Executive Officer
CFO - Chief Financial Officer
CFTC - Commonwealth Fund for Technical Cooperation
CGI - Chartered Governance Institute
CIMA - Chartered Institute of Management Accountants
CIPE - Centre for International and Private Enterprises
CoC - Codes of Conduct
CoE -Codes of Ethics
CSR - Corporate Social Responsibility
DOSE – Directorate of State Enterprises
EU - European Union
FDI - Foreign Direct Investment
FINDECO – Finance and Development Corporation
GCGF - Global Corporate Governance Forum
GDP - Gross Domestic Product
GRZ - Government of the Republic Zambia
GTZ - German Organisation for Technical Cooperation
ICSA - Institute of Chartered Secretaries and Administrators
ICT - Information and Communication Technologies
IDC - Industrial Development Corporation
IDM - Investment and Debt Management
IFC - International Finance Corporation
ILF - International Leadership Foundation
IMF - International Monetary Fund
INDECO – Industrial Development Corporation
IoDZ - Institute of Directors Zambia
LuSE - Lusaka Securities Exchange (formerly Lusaka Stock Exchange)

MD - Managing Director

MINDECO – Mining Development Cooperation and Development

MMD - Movement for Multiparty Democracy

NCCM- Nchanga Consolidated Copper Mines

NEPAD – New Partnership for Africa's Development

NGO - Non-Governmental Organisation

OECD - Organisation of Economic Cooperation and Development

PACRA - Patents and Companies Registration Agency

PESTEL – Political, Economic, Social, Technological, Environmental and Legal analysis

PF - Patriotic Front

PSAG - Private Sector Advisory Group

PSDP - Private Sector Development Programme

RCM - Roan Consolidated Mines

SADC -Southern African Development Community

SIDA - Swedish International Development Cooperation Agency

SME - Small and Medium Enterprises

SOE - State Owned Enterprises

SWOT - Strengths, Weaknesses, Opportunities and Threats

DFID - United Kingdom Department for International Development

UN - United Nations

UNDP - United Nations Development Programme

UNIP - United National Independence Party

USAID - United States Agency for International Development

ZAMPOST – Zambia Postal Service Corporation

ZAMTEL –Zambia Telecommunications Company

ZANACO – Zambia National Commercial Bank

ZCCM-IH – Zambia Consolidated Copper Mines – Investments Holdings

ZDA - Zambia Development Agency

ZESCO - Zambia Electricity Supply Corporation

ZICTA – Zambia Information and Communications Technology Authority

ZIL - Zambian Institute of Leadership

ZIMCO – Zambia Industrial and Mining Corporation

ZNBC - Zambia National Broadcasting Corporation

ZPA - Zambia Privatisation Agency

APPENDICES

ADDRESS BY HIS HONOUR THE VICE PRESIDENT OF THE
REPUBLIC OF ZAMBIA, LT. GENERAL CHRISTON TEMBO TO THE
FIRST WORKSHOP ON CORPORATE GOVERNANCE ORGANISED
BY THE COMMONWEALTH SECRETARIAT IN ASSOCIATION
WITH COMMONWEALTH ASSOCIATION FOR CORPORATE
GOVERNANCE AND THE INSTITUTE OF CHARTERED
SECRETARIES AND ADMINISTRATORS (ZAMBIA ASSOCIATION)
ON 22ND JUNE 1998 AT HOTEL INTERCONTINENTAL, LUSAKA

Mr. Chairman
Distinguished Guests
Ladies and Gentlemen

It is with great pleasure and delight that I welcome all distinguished Guests and
Resource Personnel who have come to Zambia to share with us experiences
on Corporate Governance practiced in other Commonwealth member states.

It is also fitting that I should express my profound appreciation and gratitude
to the Commonwealth Secretariat and the Commonwealth Association
for Corporate Governance to have been able to organise the workshop of
such magnitude in Zambia in conjunction with the Institute of Chartered
Secretaries and Administrators (Zambia Association) I would like to say to
you all that – well done.

The workshop that is being conducted in Lusaka was borne out of the
heads of Government meeting in Edinburgh in October 1997 when it was
decided to establish a Commonwealth Association for Corporate Governance
(CACG). The CACG was mainly established to promote best practice in
Corporate Governance throughout the Commonwealth to achieve more
effective economic and social development through information sharing and
exchange of experience.

Mr. Chairman, distinguished Guests, Ladies and Gentlemen, the workshop in Lusaka seeks to achieve three broad objectives. Firstly, it will lay the foundation for the promotion of the ideals of Corporate Governance in Zambia.

Secondly, it will provide a forum for participants to determine what the best practice is for Corporate Governance in Zambia. Thirdly, the workshop will facilitate the development of institutional capacities for good Corporate Governance in Zambia.

Mr. Chairman, the workshop in Lusaka could not have come at any better time than now when the economy of Zambia has been liberalised and most of the companies have been privatised.

When the MMD Government assumed office in 1991, we set out to implement a Macro-Economic Reform programme which was aimed in the first instance at stabilising the economy. The attainment of Macro-Economic stability was rightly considered an essential condition for regenerating foreign private sector interest in this country and as well as laying the foundation for future sustainable growth. Today, Zambia is one of Africa's most open and private sector led economies.

Secondly, we sought to remove all legal impediments to free and private sector participation. All existing monopolistic laws were repealed and in their place a legal framework which ensured a free and open economy was enacted. Government sought to disengage itself from business and restricted it role to that of creating a positive business and environment in which the private sector could thrive. My alluding to the Macro-Economic Reform and the legal framework is mainly to convey one important message. The message is that our Government will fully support practices aimed at generating investment in this country.

Mr Chairman, I am glad that it is the private sector who are aiming at self-regulating their own practices in board rooms for the benefit of the investors. The public and our Government, I say I am glad because the best practice in board rooms could only be done by the private sector and not the Government. Our *Government had done and will continue doing its part of the Macro-Economic Reform programme including the privatisation of the remaining enterprises and as a result the remaining board room space for the Government will disappear. The board room will become a restricted area to Government. This way state control or influence will disappear. This was the vision of the MMD Government.*

Mr. Chairman, it is equally gratifying to learn that one of the final results of this workshop will be to set up an Institute of Directors in Zambia. The MMD Government is fully supporting of this move, for it is through the establishment of an Independent Institute that the Corporate Governance will be promoted in Zambia. The MMD Government stands ready to support you in every way possible to create such an Institute like yesterday! In particular the MMD Government is in a hurry to create positive environment to attract foreign investment in the country. It is, therefore, in the context that we see the running of the workshop in Lusaka as being timely and coincides well with MMD Government divestiture programme.

Mr. Chairman, may I now turn to the role of the Professional Administrators of Corporate Governance in companies - the Chartered Company Secretaries, I am aware that the Institute of Chartered Secretaries and Administrators is the only professional body which provides specific training in the area of Corporate Governance in their course of Company Secretarial practice. With the liberalised economy and with the participation of private sector in the economy the Chartered Company Secretaries now face enormous challenges in their profession, as Chief Administrative Officers of the companies and other corporate bodies. They will be required to rise to challenges of their profession so as to be able to advise boards and their respective chairmen and Chief Executives on matters of Corporate Governance.

Mr Chairman, it need to be mentioned that, for a long time to be specific 25 years or so. The role of Chartered Company Secretaries in Boards and Management was watered down by the previous UNIP Administration. The reason was that most appointments were purely based on the political allegiance to the party in Government at the time. To this end, Chairmen, Directors, Chief Executive and Company Secretaries were appointed based on political allegiance to the ruling party at the time.

Mr. Chairman, distinguished guests and ladies and gentlemen, you will no doubt agree that poor performance of State Owned Enterprises was largely due to incompetence of boards, management and political interference. It is for this reason that the MMD government decided upon a policy of privatisation which would ensure transfer of management roles and ownership to competent and qualified personnel.

Mr. Chairman, Corporate Governance is not a subject restricted to Company Administration. Corporate Governance is equally applicable to Government organisations and boards, such as Universities, Colleges, Health Boards, Water Boards, Examination Council, Environment Council and such Corporate Institutions. All these Government aided organisation and institutions require good Corporate Governance practices so as to ensure efficient and effective management of resources. It is important that the philosophy of good Corporate Governance should be applied in all sectors of the economy.

Mr. Chairman, I would like to conclude by saying that the workshop should attempt to highlight distinct roles of Chairmen, Directors, Chief Executives and Company Secretaries and the relationship of these functions in terms of efficient Corporate Governance in board and organisations.

Mr. Chairman, I would like to wish you and all participants, success in the deliberations. I therefore declare the workshop open.

THANK YOU

WORKSHOP ON CORPORATE GOVERNANCE
ORGANISED BY THE COMMONWEALTH SECRETARIAT IN
ASSOCIATION WITH COMMONWEALTH ASSOCIATION FOR
CORPORATE GOVERNANCE AND THE INSTITUTE OF CHARTERED
SECRETARIES AND ADMINISTRATORS (ZAMBIA ASSOCIATION)
22,23,24 JUNE 1998 HOTEL INTERCONTINENTAL, LUSAKA

			PROGRAMME
			22 June 1998
08:00	-	08:50	Registration
09:00			Arrival of the Guest of Honour, His Honour The Vice President of the Republic of Zambia, **Lt. Gen. Christon Tembo, MP**
09:05	-	10:00	Welcome Remarks, Official Opening, Vote of Thanks
10:00	-	10:30	Morning Tea
10:30	-	12:00	Policy Issues and Strategic Planning **Michael Gillibrand**
12:00	-	13:00	Lunch
13:00	-	14:00	Corporate Governance – A Commonwealth Perspective **Geoffrey Bowes**
14:00	-	15:00	Corporate Governance – An African Perspective **Boyman Mancama**
15:00	-	15:30	Afternoon Tea
15:30	-	16:30	Corporate Governance – An Investor's Perspective **Matthew Durdy**
16:30	-	17:30	General Discussion

			23 June 1998
09:00	-	13:00	Workshops for Company Chairmen ***Geoffrey Bowes*** Non-executive Directors ***Boyman Mancama*** Chief Executive Officers ***Michael Gillibrand*** Company Secretaries ***Rodney Rawlinson***
13:00	-	14:00	Lunch
14:00	-	15:00	Compliance with Local Laws ***M.C.J. Kunkuta & Harriet T. Sikasote***
15:30	-	15:30	Afternoon Tea
15:30	-	17:30	Discussion and Resolution on Best Practice
17:30	-	18:30	Closure

			24 June 1998
09:00	-	10:00	An Institute to Promote Corporate Governance - A Commonwealth Perspective **Geoffrey Bowes**
10:00	-	10:30	Morning Tea
10:30	-	12:00	Institutions in Africa Promoting Corporate Governance ***Boyman Mancama & Rodney Rawlinson***
12:00	-	13:00	Lunch
13:00	-	14:00	Syndicate Discussion
14:00	-	15:00	Report Back
15:00	-	15:30	Afternoon Tea
15:30	-	16:30	Resolution on What to Do
16:30	-	17:00	Official Closing by the Minister of Commence, Trade and Industry

LIST OF NAMES OF PEOPLE WHO ATTENDED THE 1ST WORKSHOP ON CORPORATE GOVERNANCE AT INTERCONTINENTAL HOTEL ON 24TH JUNE, 1998.

No.	Title	Surname	First Name	Designation	Organisation
1.	Mr.	Akapelwa	Simomo S.	Managing Director	Zambia National Insurance Brokers Limited
2.	Mr.	Bannatyane	I.C	Managing Director	TZI
3.	Ms.	Bbuku	Theresa	Board Secretary	Zambia National Broadcasting Corporation
4.	Dr.	Beele	Ernest M.	Lecturer/Dean of Students	Copperbelt University
5.	Mr.	Chibesakunda	K.N	Chairman	Zambia National Broadcasting Corporation
6.	Ms.	Chifungula	Anna	Controller of Internal Audit	Ministry of Finance & Economic Development
7.	Ms.	Chikoye	G. M	Director of Audits	Office of the Auditor General
8.	Mr.	Chinunka	Webby M.E	Chief Internal Auditor	Ministry of Finance H/Q
9.	Mr.	Chisanga	Patrick D.	Executive Chairman	Muchanga Investments Limited
10.	Ms.	Cifire-Tembo	Angela	Snr Mgr Change, Corporate Planning & Int R	Zambia Electricity Supply Corporation

11.	Mr.	Daka	Michael M.	Director	Zambia Institute of Mass Communication
12.	Mr.	Gulati	Satish Kumar	Deputy Director	Zambia Centre for Accountancy Studies
13.	Mr.	Hamunjele	Maulu	Inspector	Bank of Zambia-Financial Systems Supervision
14.	Mrs.	Jere	Elizabeth Banda	Manager	Zambia Privatisation Agency
15.	Mr.	Kakoma	Charles	Managing Editor	Zambia Daily Mail Limited
16.	Mr.	Kalaba	Emmanuel Kunda	Senior I nvestigations Officer	Anti-Corruption Commission
17.	Mr.	Kalaluka	Ken	Human Resources Manager	Zambia National Provident Fund
18.	Ms.	Kalimamukw-ento	Musonda	Assistant Company Secretary	Chilanga Cement PLC
19.	Mr.	Kapambwe	J.		Copperbelt University
20.	Mr.	Kapilikisha	F.C	Deputy Company Secretary	Zambia Consolidated Copper Mines
21.	Mr.	Kapumpa	Mumba S.	Secretary & Chief Executive	Securities & Exchange Commission
22.	Mr.	Kasaka	Field C.	Finance Manager/ Company Secretary	Zambia National Holdings Limited

23.	Mr.	Kasongo	Kamfwa	Corporation Secretary	Zambia State Insurance Corporation
24.	Mr.	Kataya	Stephen	Business Planning Manager	Zambia Electricity Supply Corporation Limited
25.	Mr.	Lubinda	J.M	Company Secretary	National Airports Corporation Limited
26.	Mr.	Lukashi	Fabiano Chipasha	Team Leader, Post Privatisation	Zambia Privatisation Agency
27.	Mr.	Lukhele	Jorge	Assistant Director	Department of Human Resource Development
28.	Mr.	Manjeese	Noah	General Manager – Administration & Finance	Intermarket Discount (Z) Limited
29.	Mr.	Mbewe	Luke C.	Managing Director	ERZ (Holdings) Limited
30.	Ms.	Moono	Dorothy Kapambala	Registrar	Barclays Bank Zambia Limited
31.	Ms.	Mooya	Flora Kantu	Board Secretary	Local Authority Supernuation Fund
32.	Dr.	Mpuku	Herrick C.	Lecturer	Copperbelt University
33.	Mr.	Mufaya	S.L	Management Consultant	Coopers & Lybrand
34.	Mrs.	Mulenga	Regina M.K	Chief Accountant	Zambia Privatisation Agency

35.	Mr.	Mulevu	M.B	Chief Internal Auditor	Zambia Privatisation Agency
36.	Mr.	Mumba	J.M	Commercial Manager	Zambia National Oil Company
37.	Mr.	Munsele	Derick F.	Team Leader	Zambia Privatisation Agency
38.	Mr.	Musuku	Benjamin	Inspector	Bank of Zambia Financial System Supervision
39.	Mr.	Mutambo	Stephen	Managing Consultant	Contact Management Systems
40.	Ms.	Muwo	Joyce	Manager, Administration / Company Secretary	Zambia National Oil Company Limited
41.	Ms.	Mwale	Margaret V.	Director	KPMG
42.	Mr.	Mwambwa	R.M	Acting Director of Audits	Audit office
43.	Ms.	Mweemba	Sheila	Assistant Registrar	Zambia Consolidated Copper Mines Limited
44.	Ms.	Ncube	Mary	Chief Executive	MTN Special Engagements
45.	Mr.	Ndhlovu	Stephen	Company Secretary	Zambia Privatisation Agency
46.	Ms.	Ng'andu	Suzyo Musukwa	Secretarial Officer	ZCCM Limited
47.	Ms.	Ng'andu	Kayobo A.M	Deputy Director	Anti-Corruption Commission

48.	Mr.	Ngoma	Godwin C.	Public Relations & Development Manager	Indo-Zambia Bank Limited
49.	Mr.	Nsama	Gilbert	Chief Accountant	United Quarries Limited
50.	Mr.	Pankratz	David	Incoming Generating Consultant	Mennonite Central Committee
51.	Mr.	Phiri	Abel A.	Managing Director	Zambia State Insurance Corporation
52.	Mr.	Ponde	Isaac M.	Chief Administrative Officer	Zambia Privatisation Agency
53.	Mr.	Richards	Tony	Water Sector Programme Co-ordinator	GTZ
54.	Mr.	Shawa	Willie	Managing Director	Lusaka Water & Sewerage Company
55.	Mr.	Siame	Frederick Musipi	Auditor General	Office of Auditor General
56.	Mr.	Sichombo	D.M	Company Secretary	Lusaka Water & Sewerage Company Limited
57.	Mr.	Soko	R.N	Managing Director	Chipata Water & Sewerage Company
58.	Ms.	Sombe	Betty	Director Corporate Development	Zambia Electricity Supply Corporation
59.	Mrs.	Syafunko	Pitcaim	Finance Director	Consolidated Tyre Services Limited

60.	Mr.	Theu	J.B	Board Secretary	Zambia National Provident Fund
61.	Mr.	Thomas	Mohan	Financial Manager	Macmed Zambia Limited
62.	Mr.	Zulu	Peter T.	Chief Internal Auditor	Ministry of Finance & Economic Development
63.	Mr.	Zulu	George	Company Secretary	Zambia Electricity Supply Corporation Limited

APPENDIX 4

INSTITUTE OF DIRECTORS
IN ZAMBIA
(In Formation)

ARTICLES OF ASSOCIATION OF THE INSTITUTE OF DIRECTORS, A
COMPANY LIMITED BY GUARANTEE

NAME AND AFFILIATION

a. The name of the Institute shall be the Institute of Directors in Zambia, hereafter referred to as "the institute".

b. The Institute shall be affiliated to the Institute of Directors in London, incorporated by Royal Charter in the United Kingdom and have cooperation with the Institute of Directors in Southern Africa and the Institute of Directors in Zimbabwe.

ARTICLES OF ASSOCIATION

2.1 The Institute shall be a voluntary association of persons, incorporated, non-profit making, the membership of which shall be restricted to persons who are admitted to membership of the Institute in terms of these Articles of Association.

OBJECTS

3.0 THE objects for which the Institute is established shall be to provide a local organisation in Zambia for its members with the following particularised objects:

3.1 To promote excellence in corporate governance,to represent interests of directors and facilitate their professional development in support of the economic well-being of Zambia.

3.2 To enhance the standards and effectiveness of Directors through information and education on their legal, moral, financial and general rights and responsibilities in respect of their companies, shareholders, employees, management and the community as a whole.

3.3 To inculcate the highest standard of ethics amongst Directors.

3.4 To provide an effective voice for company directors in public affairs and for that purpose to take a continuing and effective interest in legislation, economic and social matters and the law generally to ensure the preservation of basic commercial freedom and to prevent abuse of such freedom.

3.5 To uphold and maintain the concept of corporate entity, the principle of limited liability and the preservation and furtherance of the free enterprises system.

3.6 To acknowledge the complementary contribution to the economy made by both large and small businesses.

3.7 To promote interest in the Institute and its objects, in particular to promote, establish and maintain branches of the Institute, to carry out the objects and conduct of the local affairs of the Institute and to promote, establish and maintain and, or control committees and other forms of organisations and administration for the purpose of enlarging the influence and operation of the Institute.

3.8 To co-operate with other parties and organisations whether they be domiciled within or outside Zambia provided they have objects in whole or in part similar to the objects of the Institute.

3.9 To plan, arrange, sponsor and conduct training courses relating to the duties and responsibilities of company directors and all manner of subjects relating to the direction of companies which are for the improvement of and benefit to company directors.

3.10 To conduct seminars, conferences, workshops and every form of lecture or discussion relating to any business matters falling within the scope of companies' activities.

3.11 To publish and disseminate pamphlets, discussion papers and other documents associated with the affairs and activities of the Institute.

3.12 To arrange and hold social functions for members of the Institute and their guests.

3.13 To observe, uphold and further objects and purposes of the Institute.

3.14 To retain its affiliation with the Institute of Directors in London.

POWERS

4.0 For the better attainment of its objects the Institute shall be empowered:

4.1 To establish, subsidise, promote, co-operate with, receive into union or affiliation, subscribe and donate to or become a member of, control, manage, superintend, lend or give monetary assistance to, or otherwise aid associations, institutions and organisations incorporated or not incorporated and whether within Zambia or elsewhere provided they have objects substantially similar to the objects set out in Rule hereof.

4.2 For the purpose of furthering the objects of theInstitute to raise money by all lawful means and to solicit, receive, and enlist financial or other aid from individuals, trusts, companies, corporations, associations, societies, institutions and other organisations or authorities and to conduct fund - raising campaigns.

4.3 To make known and further the objects and activities of the Institute by the publications and distribution of papers, journals and other publications and by making the same known by any means thought to be convenient and desirable.

4.4 To open, operate and close accounts at Banks, Building Societies, and other registered financial institutions and draw, make, accept, endorse, discount, execute and issue promissory notes, bills of exchange, warrants and other negotiable instruments.

4.5 To borrow and raise money for any of the purpose of the Institute and to secure the payment thereof in such manner as may be lawful including, without prejudice to the generality of the foregoing, by any mortgage, charge or debenture upon or over all or any of the property of the Institute present or future.

4.6 To invest and deal with the money of the Institute:

(i)   to purchase, take on lease, licence or in exchange, have or acquire by gift or otherwise, movable and immovable property of any nature or description;

(ii)   to sell or otherwise dispose of such property or exchange it for other property;

(iii) to let or lease such property for such terms at such rent and upon such conditions as may be deemed to be desirable;

(iv) to raise money on such property on such terms and conditions as may be deemed to be desirable;

(v) to construct, maintain and alter any buildings or premises necessary or convenient for the purposes of the Institute;

(vi) to sell, improve, manage, develop, exchange, lease, mortgage, place under option, dispose of, turn to account or otherwise deal with, either absolutely, conditionally, or for any limited interest, all or any part of the property and assets of the Institute for such consideration as the Institute may think fit, with power on any sale to allow any time or times for the payment of the whole or any part of the purchase money arising from such sale either with or without security.

4.7   To promote interest in the Institute and its objects.

4.8   To undertake and execute any trusts the undertaking whereof may be necessary or desirable for the carrying out of any of the objects of the Institute, and to accept any gift, endowment or bequest made to the Institute generally, or for the purpose of any specific object and to carry out any trusts attached to any gift, endowment or bequest provided that the institute shall only deal with any property which is subject to any trust or trusts in such manner as is allowed by law having regard to such trust or trusts.

4.9   From time to time to make, amend and, or repeal bye-laws in accordance with these Rules for the purposes herein mentioned.

4.10 To organise and support or assist in organising and supporting conferences, discussions, lectures, meetings and the reading of papers on matters of interest or benefit to the members of the Institute or which may assist in the attainment or advancement or any of the objects of the Institute.

4.11 To employ the services of, or consult individuals or bodies corporate or unincorporated, expert in any of the fields in which the Institute or its members are or may be interested, to delegate to such individuals or bodies the performance of all or any of the functions of the Institute and to pay for and make use of the knowledge, information or services thus obtained in any manner whatsoever.

4.12 To act as adviser or consultants in respect of any of the above matters to any of the members of the Institute or other persons or bodies operating with similar objects within Zambia.

4.13 To appoint a Chief Executive, Secretary and such other officials as it considers are required, and to settle the terms of such appointments and the duties of the appointees none of whom need be a member of the Institute.

4.14 To engage or employ such other personnel and to pay them in return for such services provided for the Institute, fees, salaries, wages, gratuities and, or pensions.

4.15 To recompense or reimburse any members of the Board of Directors or Management of the Institute for any travelling or other expenses incurred by such members in connection with the affairs of the Institute in terms of any specific assignment initiated by the Board of Directors or Management, as the case may be and with the Institute when such award is judged to be deserved and appropriate.

4.16 To participate in and enjoy benefits and financial advantage for members by being affiliated to the Institute.

4.17 To appoint Directors of the Institute.

4.18 To institute and defend any legal proceedings brought by or against the Institute.

4.19 Generally to do all such acts, matters and things and to enter into and make such agreements as are incidental or conducive to the attainment of any of the objects of the Institute.

4.20 If upon the winding up or dissolution of the Institute there remains after the satisfaction of all its debts and liabilities any property whatsoever the same shall not be paid to or distributed among the members of the Institute but shall be given or transferred to some other Institute, society or body having objects similar to the objects of the Institute and which shall prohibit the distribution of its income and property among its members upon a winding up or dissolution, such institute, society or other body to be determined by the members of Institute at or before the time of dissolution and if effect cannot be given to the afore said provision then for some charitable object.

INTERPRETATION

5. Any matters not provided for in these Articles or any question arising as to the interpretation of these articles shall be decided by the Board of Directors, as hereinafter defined. At any General Meeting any such questions shall be decided by the President whose ruling shall be final. Subject to the foregoing, in these Articles:

   (a) "the Act" means the Companies Act Chapter 388 of the Laws of Zambia;

   (b) "Annual General Meeting" as defined in Article 23;

(c)   "Associate Member" as defined in Annex A;

(d)   "Branches" as permitted in Article 61.1;

(e)   "By-Laws" as permitted in Article 61.2;

(f)   "Centres as permitted in Article 61.1;

(g)   "Code as permitted in Article 79

(h)   "the Chief Executive" means the person appointed Chief Executive pursuant to Article 62 hereof;

(i)   "the Board" means the Board of Directors of the Institute as a body or a quorum of the members thereof at a Board Meeting;

(j)   "Board Member" means a member who is appointed or elected to the Board pursuant to these Articles;

(k)   "Directors" as defined in the Companies Act Chapter 388 of the Laws of Zambia;

(l)   "Extraordinary General Meeting" as defined in Article 24 and 25;

(m)   "Fellow" and includes Honorary Fellow as defined in Annex A;

(n)   "the Institute" means the Institute of Directors in Zambia;

(o) "Member" and includes Honorary Member as defined in Annex A;

(p) "Zambia" means The Republic of Zambia;

(q) "Office" means the registered office for the time being of the Institute;

(r) "Officer" as defined in Article 41.1 (a)

(s) "President" means the person elected President from time to time pursuant to Article 41;

(t) "retired" as defined in Annex A;

(u) "the Seal" means the Common Seal of the Institute;

(v) "Secretary" means the Secretary of the Institute;

(w) "sub-Committee" means a subcommittee or committee constituted under Article 56;

(x) "Vice President" means the person elected Vice President from time to time pursuant to Article 41.3.(ii)

Words and Expressions contained in these articles shall be interpreted in accordance with the provisions of the Interpretation and General Provisions Chapter 2 of the Laws of Zambia.

6. THE members of the Institute shall be the subscribers to the application for the incorporation of the Institute under the Companies Act Chapter 388 of the Laws of Zambia together

with such other persons as the Board shall admit to membership from time to time and such subscribers and every person admitted to membership of the Institute shall be deemed to have agreed to be bound by these Articles and by any other Rules, Regulations or By-Laws of the Institute from time to time in force.

7. ANY persons, who in the opinion of the Board, are persons engaged in or otherwise interested in the supervision and direction of a company, corporation, trust body corporate, statutory body, state owned enterprise, local authority or similar body at director or similar level in Zambia shall be eligible to apply for membership.

8. THE Board shall have power to create different categories within the membership and may recommend different rates of annual subscription for each category if it so desires. The Board shall be empowered to determine these categories upon whatever basis it thinks is proper in the circumstances, however the normal categories will be:

> Fellow
>
> Associate
>
> Honorary

QUALIFICATIONS for these are shown in Annex A.

9. ONLY Members and Fellows have powers to vote and be officers of the Institute pursuant to these Articles.

10. Every applicant for membership shall apply on an appropriate form supplied by the Institute.

11. At the next meeting of the Board (and as soon as possible) after the receipt of any application for membership, such application shall be considered by the Board who shall either, at that meeting or at the next subsequent meeting determine upon the admission or rejection of the applicant PROVIDED HOWEVER that the Board may delegate the task of considering applications for membership to a sub-committee which shall have power to determine the applications.

12. When an applicant has been accepted for membership the Secretary of the Institute shall forthwith send to the applicant written notice of acceptance and a request for payment of the entrance fee and first annual subscription. Upon payment thereof the applicant shall be sent a membership card and shall thereupon become a member of the Institute within the category there stated provided that if payment of the entrance fee and subscription or either of them, are not paid within two calendar months after the date of the said notice the Institute may in its discretion cancel its acceptance of the applicant for membership of the Institute.

13. Whenever an application for membership is accepted within the last six months of the Institute's financial year the applicant shall pay one half of the annual subscription.

14. Notwithstanding the election procedure desired in this Rule any member of the Institute or any Institute of Directors throughout the world affiliated to the IOD (referring to as a reciprocal member) may apply for membership of the Institute giving details of his reciprocal membership and the Executive Committee shall admit him to membership of the Institute upon payment of annual subscription, or part thereof, but awaiting the entrance fee.

CESSATION OF MEMBERSHIP

15. The membership of the Institute shall cease:

15.1 If the member resigns by notice in writing left at or sent by post to the Institute.

15.2 If a majority of three-quarters of those Board Members present and voting at a meeting of the Board by resolution terminate the membership of any member whose conduct, in their opinion, has compromised the position of the Institute or brought the Institute into disrepute to Rule 77, breached the Rule 78, or has breached any code published by the Board pursuant to Rule 79, such person shall from the time of such resolution cease to be a member of the Institute, provided that before such resolution is proposed such member shall have at least twenty one (21) days prior notice of such resolution and shall have the right to be heard at the meeting at which it is proposed.

15.3 If the membership is terminated under Article 16.

15.4 If:-

(i) the member dies;

(ii) the member becomes disqualified to hold the office of director of a company by virtue of the operation of any act or statutory regulation;

(iii) the member becomes bankrupt;

(iv) the member becomes prohibited from being a director by reason of any order made under the Companies Act Chapter 388 of the Laws of Zambia or any Acts passed in substitution or any corresponding provision passed in substitution therefor;

(v)   the member becomes of unsound mind or becomes the subject of any order made under the provisions of the Protection of Personal and Property Rights Act 1988.

16. AND any member resigning from the Institute or for any other reason ceasing to be a Member shall not be entitled to any refund of subscription or any part thereof.

1.If a member fails to pay any subscription or levy or other sum of money whatsoever due by the member for period of three (3) calendar months after it becomes due then the Board may, at any time while the sum remains unpaid, terminate the membership of that member.

2.A member whose membership is terminated pursuant to this Rule may be reinstated upon such terms as the Board may determine.

17. A member whose membership ceases in any manner shall remain liable to the Institute for all subscriptions, levies and other moneys whatsoever due prior to the termination of the membership (including the subscription payable in respect of the period current at the date of such termination).

HONORARY MEMBERSHIP

18. NOTWITHSTANDING anything elsewhere herein contained the members may elect, at general meetings, persons to be Honorary members who have rendered outstanding service to the Institute. Honorary members shall have the same rights and duties as members but shall not be liable for any subscriptions or any other fees that may be imposed.

MEMBERS' SUBSCRIPTIONS

19. THE amount of the annual subscription payable to members shall be determined by the Board. The Board shall have the power to discount a rebate in respect of subscriptions paid by a nominated date, such date and the amount of the rebate to be determined by the Board.

20. IN the case of persons whose applications for membership is accepted pursuant to Rule 11, the first annual subscription shall be payable as provided in Rule 10. In all other cases annual subscription shall be payable in advance by the first day of February in each year or such later date as the Board shall determine from time to time.

21. NOTWITHSTANDING the provisions of Rule 12 and 20, if the date of admission of a member falls within one of the periods specified in this rule annual subscription payable by that member shall be that proportion of the annual subscription payable for that year by members as is set out against that period.

1st July to 30th September	one half
1st October to 31st December	one quarter

22. THE Board may, with the authority of a resolution passed by the Institute in general meeting by notice to the members, impose a levy on the members of such per member and payable at such time or times as is authorised by the resolution; provided that the annual subscription payable by that member in respect of that year. The amount of a levy made in accordance with this Rule shall be debt due to the Institute by each member upon whom the levy is imposed within thirty (30) days after the service upon the member of the notice referred to in the first sentence of this Rule.

GENERAL MEETINGS

23. A general meeting of the Institute to be called the "Annual General Meeting" shall, in addition to any other meeting, be held at least once in every subsequent calendar year and not more than fifteen (15) months after the holding of the last preceding Annual General Meeting.

24. All general meetings other than the Annual General Meeting shall be called Extraordinary General Meetings.

25. THE President or any five (5) members of the Board may, convene an Extraordinary General Meeting. An Extraordinary General Meeting shall be convened on such requisition.

26. SUBJECT to the provisions of the Act relating to special resolutions and agreements for shorter notice not less than fourteen (14) days' notice (exclusive of the day which the notice is served or deemed to be served but inclusive of the day for which notice is given) specifying the place, the day and the hour of meeting and in case of special business, the general nature of that business shall be given to such persons as are entitled to receive such notices from the Institute.

27. ALL business shall be special that is transacted at an Extraordinary General Meeting and also all that is transacted at an Annual General Meeting with the exception of the consideration of the accounts, balance sheets and the report of the Board and Auditor, and the appointment of members of the Board in place of those retiring and the approving of the appointment and the remuneration of the auditor.

28.

(a) THE business to be considered at an Annual General Meeting shall be:

(iii) To receive the annual accounts, the Directors report and the Auditors report;

(iv) To approve the appointment and remuneration of the Auditor,

(v)

(vi) To consider any notice of motion of which notice has been given in accordance with paragraph (b) of this Article;

(vii) Election of Board Members and

(viii) To consider any special or general business.

(b) NOTICES of motion to be presented in an Annual General Meeting shall be conflict in writing and lodged at the office not later than twenty-eight (28) days prior to the date fixed for that meeting and a copy of such notices of motion shall be sent to each Member not later than Fourteen (14) days prior to the date fixed for that meeting.

PROCEEDING AT GENERAL MEETINGS

29. SUBJECT to Article 30 no business shall be transacted at any general meeting unless a quorum of members is present. Save as herein otherwise provided any ten (10) members being entitled to vote and being present in person shall be a quorum.

30. IF within half an hour of the time appointed for the meeting a quorum is not present, the meeting, if convened upon the requisition of members, shall be dissolved, in any other case it shall stand adjourned to the same day in the same week at the same time and place, or to such other day and at such other time and place as the Board may determine and if at the adjourned meeting a quorum is not present within half an hour after the time appointed for the meeting the members present, being not less than five (5) shall be a quorum.

31. THE President shall be entitled to take the chair at every general meeting but if there is no President, or if the President is not present within 15 minutes after the time appointed for holding the meeting or is present but is unwilling to act as chairperson of the meeting, the Vice President shall be entitled to take the chair and if there is no Vice President or if the Vice President is unwilling to act as chairperson then the members eligible to vote at that meeting who are present shall choose one of their own number to be chairperson of the meeting.

32. THE chairperson of a general meeting may, with the consent of the meeting, adjourn the same from time to time and from place to place but no business shall be transacted at any adjourned meeting other than the business which was left unfinished at the meeting from which the adjournment took place. If any meeting is adjourned for more than thirty (30) days' notice of such adjournment shall be given to all the members entitled to receive notices of general meeting in the same manner as notice as, or ought to have been given, to the original meeting, but otherwise it shall not be necessary to give notice of an adjournment or of the business to be transacted at an adjourned meeting.

33. AT any general meeting of members eligible to vote at that meeting, a resolution put to the vote of the meeting shall be decided on a show of hands unless a poll is (before or on the declaration of the result of the show of hands) demanded:-

    (i)   By the chairperson; or

    (ii)   By at least three (3) members present in person or by proxy.

34. Unless a poll is so demanded a declaration by the chairperson that a resolution has on a show of hands been carried or

carried unanimously, or by a particular majority or that a resolution has been lost, an entry to that effect in the book containing the minutes of the proceedings of the Institute shall be conclusive evidence of the fact without proof of the number or proportion of the votes recorded in favour of or against the resolution. The demand for a poll maybe withdrawn.

35. If a poll is duly demanded it shall be taken in such manner and either at once or after an interval or adjournment or otherwise as the chairperson directs. The result of the poll shall be the resolution of the meeting at which the poll was demanded. Notwithstanding the foregoing a poll demanded on the election of a chairperson or on a question of adjournment shall be taken forthwith.

36. IN the case of an equality of votes whether on a show of hands or on a poll, the chairperson of the meeting at which the show of hands takes place or at which the poll is demanded shall be entitled to a second or casting vote.

37. A member is entitled to vote in person or by proxy. On a show of hands every member present who is entitled to vote shall have one (1) vote. On a poll every member who is entitled to vote and is present in person or by proxy shall have one (1) vote.

38. A member who is entitled to attend and vote at any general meeting of the Institute may appoint another member who is similarly entitled to attend and vote for him. Notice of appointment of a proxy shall be in writing, signed by the member making the appointment and shall be lodged with the office not less than 48 hours before the time fixed for the meeting in respect of which the appointment is made.

39. No member whose annual subscription shall be more than one (1) month in arrears at the date of the meeting shall be entitled to vote at any general meeting.

40. No objection may be to the validity of any vote except at the meeting or poll at which the vote was tendered and every vote not allowed at such meeting or poll shall be deemed valid. In case of any dispute as to the admission or rejection of a vote the chairperson of the meeting shall determine the same and such determination made in good faith shall be final and conclusive.

BOARD AND OFFICERS

41. THE supervision of the management and control of the affairs of the Institute shall be vested in the Board which (in addition to any other powers and authorities expressly conferred upon the Board by these Articles) may carry into effect all or any of the objects of the Institute and may exercise all powers of the Institute and do all such acts and things as may be exercised or done by the Institute in general meeting, subject nevertheless to the provisions of these Rules and to the resolutions of the Institute in general meetings, but no such resolution shall invalidate any prior act of the Board which would have been valid had that resolution not been passed.

41.1 THE Board shall consist of:

i.   The officers of the Institute appointed as hereinafter provided; and

ii.   Board Members elected as hereinafter provided.

41.2 ONLY persons who are Fellows or Members of the Institute shall be eligible to be appointed as a board member. Such appointments will be effective from the Annual General Meeting of the Institute.

41.3 THE Officers of the Institute shall be:

i.   The President, who shall be elected each year by the Board. The retiring President shall be eligible for re-election provided that the maximum continuous term of office for president shall be three years.

ii.   One Vice President who shall be elected each year by the Board. The retiring Vice President shall be eligible for re-election provided that the maximum continuous term of office shall be three years.

41.4 ONCE the Board has elected the President and Vice President, Board may then invite the branches, whom these officers represent, to appoint other Board Members.

42. THE performance of the functions and the exercise of the powers of the Board shall not be affected by reason of there being a vacancy in respect of any of the Officers, or in the number of members of the Board provided that the number of officers and Board Members currently holding office shall not fall below five (5).

43. IF a member of the Board;

43.1 is absent, except on leave granted by the Board, from three (3) consecutive meetings of the Board; or

43.2 is found to be of unsound mind or the members' person or estate is liable to be dealt with in accordance with the law relating to mental health in force in any place; or

43.3 wilfully fails to comply with Article 60; or

43.4 ceased to be a member of the Institute; or

43.5 dies, is convicted of an indictable offence, becomes bankrupt, applies to take the benefit of any law for the relief of bankrupt or insolvent debtors, compounds with the members' creditors or makes an assignment of property for their benefits; or

43.6 ceases to be a member of the Board by virtue of the Act or is prohibited from being a director of a company by reason of any order made under the Companies Act Chapter 388 of the Laws of Zambia or any Act amending or in substitution for that Act; then that member of the Board shall ipso facto cease to hold that office and, if the member holds the office.

44. A member of the Board may resign office by notice in writing signed by the member and left at the office. A resignation under this Rule shall take effect from the day on which the notice of resignation is left at the office or such later date as is specified in that notice.

45. THE Board may at any time and from time to time appoint a member of the Institute to be a Board Member to fill a casual vacancy in the membership of the Board. Any person so appointed shall hold office the next Annual General Meeting but shall then be eligible for reappointment. Any such appointment shall be made in such a way as to maintain the representation of branches on the Board as provided in Article 37 (c).

46. THE Institute may from time to time by a resolution passed pursuant to Article 33 or 34 at a general meeting:.

(i)   Increase or reduce the number of Board Members: and/or

(ii)   Increase or reduce the number of candidates able to be elected by each Branch under Article 41©; and/or

(iii)   Determine the number of candidate able to be appointed as Board by any new Branch or Branches established pursuant to these Rules.

47. THE Board shall hold such meetings as it considers necessary for the performance of its functions.

48. THE President may at any time and the Chief Executive at the request of the President or any two (2) other members of the Board convene a meeting of the Board. Unless members of the Board who are entitled to notice agree to the holding of a meeting at shorter notice (which agreements shall be sufficiently evidenced by the presence thereat of all Board Members or by all Board Members signing a notice to that effect) not less than seven (7) days' oral or written notice of a meeting of the Board be given to each member of the Board. In the case of written notice such notice mat be given either personally or by delivering it at or sending it by prepaid post or by telex or by facsimile transmission addressed to the member of the Board at his last known place of abode or business.

49. THE President shall be entitled to take the chair at every meeting of the Board but if there is no President or if at any meeting the President is not present within fifteen (15) minutes after the time appointed for holding the meeting or is present but is unwilling to act as chairperson of the meeting, the Vice President may take the chair and in default the Board may choose one of their number to be the chairperson of that meeting.

50. THE quorum necessary for the transaction of the business of the Board shall be four (4) or such greater number as may be fixed by the Board.

51. A meeting of the Board at which a quorum is present shall be competent to exercise all or any of the authorities, powers or discretions vested in or exercised by the Board

52. QUESTIONS arising at any meeting of the Board or of a sub-committee appointed by the Board or by any such a sub-committee shall notwithstanding that it is afterwards discovered that there was some defect in the appointment or continuance in office of such person or that person was disqualified or had vacated office or was not entitled to vote be as valid as if every person had been duly appointed and was qualified and continued to hold such office.

53. A resolution in writing signed by all the members of the Board for the time being entitled to receive notice of a meeting of the Board shall be as valid and effectual as if had been passed at a meeting of the Board duly convened and held. Any such resolution may include several documents in like form each signed by one or more members of the Board.

54. A resolution in writing signed by all the members of the Board for the time being entitled to receive notice of a meeting of the Board shall be as valid and effectual as if had been passed at a meeting of the Board duly convened and held. Any such resolution may include several documents in like form each signed by one or more members of the Board.

55. A meeting of the Board may be held by the contemporaneous linking together by telephone or television conference call of a

sufficient number of members of the Board to form a quorum provided that the following conditions are met:

(i)   All members of the Board shall be entitled to notice of a meeting by telephone and to be linked by telephone or television for the purposes of such a meeting. Notice for the purposes of this provision may be necessary to give notice to a member who is absent from Zambia.

(ii)   At the commencement of each meeting by telephone or television each member taking part in the meeting must be able to hear and be heard by each of the other members taking part and each member shall signify his or her presence for the purpose of the meeting.

55. At the Board may delegate any of its authorities, powers, discretion and duties to a sub-committee or sub-committees consisting of a member of the Board or members of the Board and may from time to time revoke, withdraw, alter or vary such delegation or the appointment of any member of a sub-committee and may appoint other members thereof.   Any sub-committee so constituted or person or persons so appointed shall in the exercise of the authorities, powers, discretion and duties so delegated conform to any Regulations or By-Laws that may from time to time be imposed by the Board.

56. AT a meeting of a subcommittee a quorum is constituted by a majority of the members of that sub-committee for the time being present at such meeting.

57. THE meetings and proceedings of any sub-committee which consists of more than one (1) member shall be governed by the provisions herein contained for regulating the meetings and proceedings of the Board so far as the same are applicable thereto and are not superseded by any Regulation or By-Law made by the Board under Article (56).

58. A member of the Board and any corporation firm or other body in which the member is directly or indirectly interested may contract with the Institute and shall be entitled to remuneration, profits and benefits as if that member were not a member of the Board and shall be counted in a quorum, shall be entitled to vote on any resolution relating to any of the foregoing matters, and may witness the affixing of the Seal of the Institute to any document related to any of the foregoing matters. Every member of the Board who is in anyway, whether directly or indirectly, interested in a contract or proposed contract with the Institute (except where such interest is apparent on the fact of the transaction or consists only of being a member or creditor of another company which is interested in a contract or proposed contract with the Institute and the interest of that member of the Board may properly be regarded as not being a material interest) shall declare the nature of the member's interest to the Board before such contract is entered into PROVIDED THAT if through a mistake or inadvertence or for any reasonable other cause of member of the Board fails to declare to the Board any matter which by this Rule is required to be declared then unless in the case of a contract or proposed contract aforesaid it is proved that such contract was unfair to the Institute or was induced by fraudulent misrepresentation on the part of that person or would contravene the provisions of these Rules such failure shall not invalidate that contract nor shall that person or any other person benefiting therefrom be held accountable for any remuneration, profit or other benefit arising there from.

59. Members of the Board, shall be entitled to be paid out of the funds of the Institute those expenses that are generally or specifically authorised by the Board. The Board may award special remuneration out of the funds of the Institute to any officer or Board Member undertaking any work additional to that usually required of a Board Member.

BRANCHES AND CENTRES

60.

60.1 THE Board shall have power to establish or approve Branches and Centres of the Institute representing members living or working in such places or areas as the Board may think appropriate.

60.2 THE members represented by each of such Branches will, subject to the provisions of sub clause 61.4 of this Rule, adopt rules or regulations as laid out in Annex B for the conduct of the affairs of that Branch and to control and manage its affairs. The Board has the power to amend and approve Branch rules or regulations.

60.3 THE Board shall have power to determine at any time that any Branch shall cease to exist with effect from a particular date. Notice of such determination shall be delivered to the chairperson or other appropriate representative of the Branch in question.

60.4 A Branch or Branch Committee shall cease to be recognised as such for the purposes of the Rules if it adopts rules or regulations or other constitutional provisions which have not previously been approved by the Board.

60.5 THE minimum number of members of each branch of the Institute shall be fifteen (15) although the Board in its absolute discretion may resolve to waive thisrequirement in particular cases if it thinks fit. Only members of the Institute shall be eligible for membership of a Branch.

60.6 SUBJECT to the prior approval of the Board a branch committee may appoint a secretary for the branch (who need not be a member of the Institute) and may agree to pay an honorarium to such secretary. The amount of such approved honorarium and all other expenses properly incurred by a Branch Committee shall be reimbursed by the Institute.

CHIEF EXECUTIVE

61. THE Board may entrust to and confer upon the Chief Executive any of the powers exercisable by the upon such terms and conditions and with such restrictions as they may consider and either collaterally with or to the exclusion of their own power and may from time to time revoke, withdraw, alter or vary all or any of those powers.

62. AFTER consultation with the President, the Chief Executive, may appoint, engage and remove such employees, staff, agents, consultants and advisers as the Chief Executive deems necessary or desirable for the purposes of the Institute. All such personnel as aforesaid shall at all times carryout their duties under the supervision and control of the Chief Executive.

63. THE BOARD may appoint a person to be the Chief Executive of the Institute on such terms and conditions as to salary fees and otherwise.

SEAL

64. THE Board shall provide for the safe custody of the seal which shall only be used by the authority of the Board authorised by the Board in that behalf and every instrument to which the seal is affixed shall be assigned by a Board Member and shall be countersigned by the Chief Executive or by a second Board Member or by some other person appointed by the Board for the purpose.

FINANCE AND ACCOUNTS

65.

65.1 THE Board shall, subject to the resolutions of the Institute in general meeting, control all funds and expenditure of the Institute.

65.2 THE Board may open and operate such bank account or accounts as it sees fit.

65.3 THE financial year of the Institute shall end on 31 December in each year. THE Board shall cause proper books of account to be kept in accordance with the regulatory requirements.

66.   THE books of accounts shall be kept at the office of the Institute or, at such other place or places as the Board thinks fit and shall always be open to the inspection of the Board.

67.   THE Board shall from time to time determine at what times and places and under what conditions or regulations the accounts or books of the Institute or any of them shall be open to the inspection of members, not being Board Members, or officers of the Institute.

68.   THE Board shall from time to time cause to be prepared and to be laid before the Institute in general meeting such income and expenditure accounts, balance sheets, group accounts (if any) and reports as are required by the Articles or are thought desirable by the Board and shall cause such accounts and balance sheets to be audited.

69. A copy of every balance sheet (including every document required by law to be annexed thereto) which is to be laid before the Institute in general meeting, together with a copy of the Auditor's report, shall not less than fourteen (14) days before the date of the meeting be sent to every member of the Institute.

APPOINTMENT OF AUDITOR
70. The Institute shall appoint an Auditor

PECUNIARY GAIN
71. No member shall receive or obtain any pecuniary gain from the property or operations of the Institute provided that members shall not be deemed to have received or obtained any pecuniary gain in any of the circumstances set out in Rule 59.

BORROWING POWER
72. THE Board shall have and may exercise all the powers of borrowing set out in Rule 4 thereof, unless the Institute in general meeting shall resolve otherwise.

NOTICES
73. A notice may be given by the Institute to any member either personally or by sending it by post to the member at the member's registered address or to the address supplied by the members to the Institute for the giving of notices. Where a notice is sent by post, service of the notice shall be deemed to be effected by properly addressing prepaying and posting a letter containing the notice and to have been effected in the case of a notice of a meeting on the day after the day of its posting and in any case at the time at which the letter would be delivered in the ordinary course of post.

74.

74.1 NOTICES of every general meeting shall be given in any manner hereinbefore authorised to:

    15.   Every member who has supplied the Institute with an address for the giving of notices; and

    16.   The Auditor or Auditors for the time being of the Institute.

74.2 No other person shall be entitled to receive notice of general meetings.

74.3 THE accidental omission to give notice of a general meeting to, or the non-receipt of any such notice by any member entitled to receive the same, or the attendance and voting at any meeting of any person subsequently found not to have been entitled so to attend and vote, or any other defect in the convening, holding or conduct of any general meeting shall not invalidate the proceedings of such general meeting.

74.4 CONVENING, holding or conducting of any general meeting shall not invalidate the proceedings of such general meeting.

OBLIGATIONS

75. OFFICERS and Members of the Board and Members of Branch Committee of the Institute may not act in a manner that compromises or is likely to compromise the position of the Institute or brings or is likely to bring the Institute into disrepute. Officers, Board Members or Branch Committees must observe the same standards dealing with information received from the Institute or acting for the Institute as would be required of any director.

76. MEMBERS should at all times take all reasonable steps to act in the best interest of the Institute.

77. THE Board may prepare Codes and publish Codes, from time to time, related to the responsibility of and action by directors. Such Codes will be binding on members of the Institute.

INDEMNITY

78. EVERY member of the Board, the Chief Executive, Auditor and other officers for the time being of the Institute shall be indemnified out of assets of the Institute against any liability arising out of the execution of the duties of the member in relation to the Institute provided that in executing such duties the Board Member, Chief Executive, Auditor or other officer shall have acted honestly, reasonably and in good faith.

AMENDMENTS TO RULES

79. THESE Rules may be amended or new rules maybe added or rules may be rescinded at any Annual General Meeting of the Institute, or any Extraordinary General Meeting called for such purpose. Notice of any intended alteration of addition to, or rescission of rules must be made in writing and received by the Chief Executive not later than two (2) calendar months prior to such meeting and copy of such notice shall be sent by the Chief Executive to each member of the Institute not later than one (1) calendar month prior to such meeting. Any resolution amending, adding to or rescinding these rules or any of them shall only be effective provided it is passed by a majority of not less than three forth of such members as being entitled so to do, vote in person or by proxy at such a General Meeting of the Institute.

WINDING UP

80.

80.1 THE Institute may be voluntarily wound up if:

(i) The Institute in Annual General Meeting or Extraordinary General meeting called for the purpose shall pass a resolution requiring the Institute to be wound up (conditional on confirmation); and

(ii) Such resolution is confirmed by a subsequent Extraordinary General Meeting called for the purpose and held not earlier than thirty (30) days after the Annual General Meeting or Extraordinary General Meeting at which such resolution is passed.

80.2 UPON the winding up of the Institute its assets (if any) shall be realised in such manner as the Institute in general meeting may determine and the proceeds and assets of the Institute, after payment of the debts of the Institute shall be distributed or disposed of in accordance with the provision of Rule 4.20 hereof as determined by any Annual General Meeting or Extraordinary General Meeting called for the purpose, but not by way of distribution to members.

BOARD MEMBERS

81. There shall be six Board Members of the Institute who shall be the President, Vice President, Board Members and the Chief Executive. All the property and assets of the Institute shall be held by the Institute. The Board Members shall be indemnified against risk and expense out of the Institute's assets.

APPENDIX 5

INSTITUTE OF DIRECTORS
LIST OF MEMBERS AS AT 10 MARCH, 2001

	MEMBER	**POSITION**	**ORGANISAT-ION**	**POSTAL ADDRESS**	**TOWN**
1.	Banda Andrew	Managing Director	Micro Savings & Credit Lines Initiative	P.O Box 410427	Kasama
2.	Bell Michael John	Managing Director	Safetech Ltd.	P.O Box 32677	Lusaka
3.	Brown Veronica Moira	General Manager	Zimco Properties Ltd.	P.O Box 31930	Lusaka
4.	Chanda Kunda Esther	Managing Director	Skynet Worldwide Express	P.O Box 37782	Lusaka
5.	Chipulu Charles	Managing Director	Lusaka Water & Sewerage Company	P.O Box 50198	Lusaka
6.	Chisanga Joe Mwansa	Executive Chairman	Fidelity Consultancy Services Ltd.	P.O Box 50544	Lusaka
7.	Chisanga Patrick Daniel	Executive Chairman	Muchanga Investments Ltd.	P.O Box 50567	Lusaka
8.	Daka Mike	Director	Zamcom	P.O Box 50386	Lusaka
9.	Fraser I.	Adviser	Zambia Privatisation Agency	P.O Box 30819	Lusaka
10.	Hamuwele E.	Senior Partner	Grant Thornton	P.O Box 30885	Lusaka

11.	Healey Richard P.	Director	Tajiri Ltd.	P.O Box 37072	Lusaka
12.	Heinz S.W	Managing Director	Dunlop Zambia	P.O Box 30781	Lusaka
13.	Kabezya Lupupa	Director - HR	Securicor	P.O Box 32914	Lusaka
14.	Kamfwa K.	Corporation Secretary	Zambia State Insurance Corp.	P.O Box 30894	Lusaka
15.	Kaminsa Bernard Mwelwa	General Manager	Zambia National Commercial Bank	P.O Box 33611	Lusaka
16.	Kasaka Field Chishala	Finance Manager/ Company Secretary	Zambian National Holdings Ltd.	P.O Box 33224	Lusaka
17.	Kombe David	Managing Director	D & C Saatchi & Saatchi	P/Bag E383	Lusaka
18.	Konie Harris Saviour	Chairman/ Chief Executive	Ziggi Insurance Company Ltd.	P.O Box 37782	Lusaka
19.	Kumar S.K	Director	Pricewater houseCoopers	P.O Box 30942	Lusaka
20.	Lukashi Fabiano		Zambia Investments Centre	P.O Box 34580	Lusaka
21.	Macleod Andrew H. Sutherland	Managing Director	Stanbic Bank Zambia Ltd.	P.O Box 31955	Lusaka
22.	Malama Godfrey	Managing Director	Zambia Daily Mail	P.O Box 31421	Lusaka
23.	Mashano Alex	Chief Executive	Mitchell Cotts (Z) Ltd.	P.O Box 71677	Ndola
24.	Mbewe Luka	Chief Executive	Zambia Export Growers Association	P.O Box 31965	Lusaka

25.	Mhango DB	Managing Director	Zambia National Holdings Ltd.	P.O Box 33224	Lusaka
26.	Mongo Chanda	Director/ Chief Executive	Small Enterprises Development Board	P.O Box 35373	Lusaka
27.	Mosho Lewis	Company Secretary	Lusaka Stock Exchange	P.O Box 34523	Lusaka
28.	Mpundu Charles	General Manager	Cavmont Merchant Bank Ld.	P.O Box 38474	Lusaka
29.	Msiska Godfrey Philip	General Manager & C.E.O	New Capital Bank PLC	P.O Box 36452	Lusaka
30.	Mtine Henry	Director Engineering	Lusaka Water & Sewerage Company	P.O Box 50198	Lusaka
31.	Mukwakwa Maxwell	Company Secretary	ZCCM Ltd.	P.O Box30048	Lusaka
32.	Musonda Samuel	Managing Director	Zambia National Commercial Bank Ltd.	P.O Box 33611	Lusaka
33.	Muwo Joy.				
34.	Mwamba C. Stanely	Director	Fairchild International Ltd.	P.O Box 32592	Lusaka
35.	Nandazi Mbita Mary	Chief Executive Officer	Micro Bankers Trust	P.O Box 51122	Lusaka
36.	Nchito Nchima	Partner	MNB	P.O Box 34207	Lusaka
37.	Ncube Mary	Chief Executive	MTN Special Engagements	P.O Box 35550	Lusaka

38.	Ndhlovu Stephen	Chairman	Institute of Directors of Zambia	P.O Box 34025	Lusaka
39.	Nduna C.F	Bank Secretary	Development Bank of Zambia	P.O Box 33955	Lusaka
40.	Nebwe Esau S.S	Chief Executive	NESS Associates Lab	P.O Box 32023	Lusaka
41.	Nsama G.	Chief Accountant	United Quarries Limited	P.O Box 31098	Lusaka
42.	O'Donnell Mark	Managing Director	Union Gold (Z) Ltd.	P.O Box 51018	Lusaka
43.	Patel Mahesh	Managing Director	Lusaka Ceramic Centre Ltd.	P.O Box 34937	Lusaka
44.	Patel Suleman Ahmed	M D / Shareholder	Zambia Skyways Ltd.	P.O Box 31530	Lusaka
45.	Phiri AA	Managing Director	Zambia State Insurance Corp	P.O Box 30894	Lusaka
46.	Phiri David Abel Ray	Chairman	Stanbic Bank Zambia Ltd.	P.O Box 31955	Lusaka
47.	Sakala Bitson	Director Finance	Lusaka Water & Sewerage Company	P.O Box 50198	Lusaka
48.	Sebastian C. Kopulande	Chairman	Setrec Steel & Wood Processing Ltd.	P.O Box 35076	Lusaka
49.	Sharma S.K	General Manager	Mulungushi Village Complex	Villa 35, Mulungushi Village	Lusaka
50.	Sichombo D.M	Director – Admin & Secretarial	Lusaka Water & Sewerage Company	P.O Box 50198	Lusaka
51.	Sikazwe Gerry	Group Chairman	Sikazwe and Company Group	P/B RW 505X, Kuluzi Mansion	Lusaka

APPENDIX 6

LIST OF THE LEADERS AND PROFESSIONALS AT ZIL LAUNCH
ON 13TH DECEMBER 2019

	Name	Organisation Represented
1	Marriot Nyangu- PhD.	The Policy and Governance Centre
2	Mary Mandiringar (Dr)	Copperstone University
3	Victoria Silutongwe	Institute of Directors - Zambia
4	Amos Simeba (Bishop)	Holiness Highway Church International
5	Nakambo Chirwa	Right to Care
6	Dokowe Newman	National Assembly of Zambia
7	Aaron Mashawo	Leaders of Tomorrow
8	Cleopatra M. Mumba	University of Zambia- Marshlands Division
9	Saka Sokontwe	Chudleigh House Schools
10	Godfrey Mumba	Motherland Enterprises
11	Prisca M. Chikwashi	Primwach Enterprises
12	Sandra Chilengi - Sakala	National Health Research Authority
13	Justine Chanda	NATSAVE
14	Engwase B. Mwale	Non-Governmental Organisations Co-ordinating Council (NGOCC) / Zambia Institute of Leadership
15	Chibamba Kanyama	Bridges Ltd/Zambian Institute of Leadership
16	Patrick D. Chisanga	Dynamic Concepts/Zambian Institute of Leadership
17	Ebby Mubanga, PhD	Teaching Council of Zambia/ Zambian Institute of Leadership
18	George Arudo	International Leadership Foundation/Zambian Institute of Leadership
19	Beatrice N. Mwila	Optimal Management

20	Petronella Chisanga	Chudleigh House School/Dynamic Concepts Ltd
21	Happy Ngoma (Rev)	Justo Mwale University
22	John Lukisa	International Leadership Foundation- Zambia
23	Irshaad Musa	The Musa Group
24	Future Mubanga	Trade Kings
25	Sandra Mulenga	Sun FM
26	Alex Machiya	DTI-Zambia
27	Reuben Chilimba	Zambia National Broadcasting Corporation -ZNBC
28	Paul Mususu (Bishop)	Evangelical Fellowship of Zambia
29	Aaron Kambikambi , Lt.	Boys Brigade
30	Maxwell Phiri	Rural Electrification Authority
32	Walusungu Nalwenga	Muvi Television
33	Chikoloi Chipopola	Muvi Television
34	Panji Nyimbili	Byta FM
35	Gerald Siingwa	Zambia National Broadcasting Corporation -ZNBC
36	Patricia Siwila	Chudleigh House Schools/Dynamic Concepts Ltd
37	Margaret Mukondwa	Dynamic Concepts Ltd
38	Nicholas Nsama Nsemiwe	Dynamic Concepts Ltd
39	Danny Sakunopa Muyunda	Dynamic Concepts Ltd
40	Norman Siwila	Dynamic Concepts/Zambian Institute of Leadership
41	Joseph Chandalala	Africa Leadership Legacy
42	Precious Mbewe	Africa Leadership Legacy
43	Likando Kapaku	Africa Leadership Legacy
44	David Kazaka	Hone FM/Life Television
45	Doreen Chembe	CBC Television
46	Jayson P. Bubala	BM Television
47	Christine M. Mayondi	LICEF Schools

48	Michael M. Chilala, PhD.	Examinations Council of Zambia
49	Brian Mushimba, (Minister)	Ministry of Higher Education
50	Mwalongo Phiri	Ministry of Higher Education

REFERENCES

Adrian Cadbury Report (1992). *The Committee on the Financial Aspects of Corporate Governance, Professional Publishing Limited, London.*

Chartered Institute of Management Accountants (2005). *Enterprise Governance: Topic Gateway Series no.32, London.*

Chipokota Mwanawansa (2016): *A Case Analysis of the Viability of the Current Regulation and Enforcement Mechanisms of Corporate Governance, University of Cape Town. (Thesis)*

G20/Organisation for Economic Cooperation and Development (2004). *OECD Principles of Corporate Governance.*

J. Sikamo, A. Mwanza and C. Mweemba (June 2016). *Copper Mining in Zambia: History and Future: The Journal of the Southern African Institute of Mining and Metallurgy. Vol.116. https//dx.doi.org/10.17159/2411-9717/2016/v116n691*
Peter Drucker (1992). Managing for the Future. Butterworth, Oxford.
Protection of Whistle Brower Act No. 4 of 2010
Report of the Committee on Parastatal Bodies on the Management and Operations of the Industrial Development Corporation in Zambia (21st September, 2017). National Assembly of Zambia.
Resolutions of Economic Affairs Committee (March, 1990). 5th National Convention of United National Independence Party (UNIP).

Taylor Karen (26th March 1990). *ZCCM-Tightening the Copperbelt: Metal Bulletin, ZCCM Looks Ahead, Southern African Economists.*

The World Factbook Zambia (Retrieved 25th February, 2018). *https//www.cia. gov/library/publications/the-world-factbook/geos/za.html.*
United Kingdom Combined Code (2006)